FUTURE-PROOFING
YOUR BUSINESS

FUTURE-PROOFING YOUR BUSINESS

REAL-LIFE STRATEGIES
TO PREPARE YOUR BUSINESS
FOR **TOMORROW, TODAY**

TROY HAZARD

WILEY

John Wiley & Sons, Inc.

Published by John Wiley & Sons, Inc., Hoboken, New Jersey.
Published simultaneously in Canada.

For general information on our other products and services or for technical support, please contact our Customer Care Department within the United States at (800) 762-2974, outside the United States at (317) 572-3993 or fax (317) 572-4002.

Wiley also publishes its books in a variety of electronic formats. Some content that appear in print may not be available in electronic books. For more information about Wiley products, visit our web site at www.wiley.com.

ISBN 978-0-470-63897-2 (cloth); ISBN 978-0-470-91845-6 (ebk);
ISBN 978-0-470-91846-3 (ebk); ISBN 978-0-470-91847-0 (ebk)

Printed in the United States of America.

10 9 8 7 6 5 4 3 2 1

To my grandmother, thank you.
I know you still watch over my future.
Mizpah Mona Blunck
1913–2009

CONTENTS

PREFACE

I t's the late 1980s. I had just opened the doors of my new consulting business when I got a call from a young bloke who advised me that he had been referred to me by a friend of mine. A fast-talking, no-nonsense voice bellows over the telephone, "I've heard you can help me with some things I need done for my business." I sheepishly respond, "Yeah, sure; what do you need?"

"Let's meet," are the next words out of this man's mouth—and the only response I get. After a brief conversation, we decide that we'll get together at an airport lounge a few days later when he will be on his way through town.

Fast-forward several days. The meeting begins with him pulling out a mile-long list of the things he wants done in his business. He prefaces the conversation by claiming, "We've got five stores now, and we're going to have 100 more; so we've got a lot of marketing stuff to get done." He finishes reading his list and poses the question, "And we're going to franchise; you've heard about franchising, right?" "Of course," I answer, while thinking to myself, "I better go buy some books on this." And after all, he didn't ask me if I had *experience* in franchising; he just wanted to know if I had *heard* of franchising.

Forty-five minutes later the meeting was coming to an end, and I had to ask the question. "So, tell me, since you need all of this stuff done and you need it all done now, can you give me an idea of what your budget is?" After a pause and some flicking of paper—as if he was looking for the magic number—he looked up and said confidently, "I've got $5,000. What do you reckon?"

At this point, I figured I had two choices. I could lie to him and say that it would all be all right, or I could tell him the truth and risk losing the business. And we really needed the business.

I chose the truth. I figured that if we were going to work together, then we might as well start the way we intended to finish—by being real and honest. So, after another short silence, I responded in a very matter-of-fact fashion: "I think we're screwed!" A slow, boyish grin came over his face as he said, "I like you. You don't speak crap." And he leaned over the table to shake my hand.

And just like that, I had my first major client—even though he didn't seem so major at the time. His name was Tom Potter. His business was Eagle Boys Pizza, and he was about to become a good friend and long-time client, as he built not 100, but over 200 stores. And my business went on to add hundreds more companies like his to our client list.

All of these great brands became part of the journey I took on the way to building a leading business consultancy. We had incredible experiences, learned wonderful things—and heard, created, and became part of some amazing stories. Along the way and over two decades, I bought and sold 10 companies and then sat back and said to myself, "One day I should write a book about all this!"

You see, I have this great job where I get to travel all over the world talking to people who run companies of all shapes and sizes. And the great gift I get from them are their stories about their businesses, lives, and the things they have done really well—and really poorly. The key thing I have learned from this experience is that at the end of the day the only way to achieve genuine success—in business and in life—is to be true and honest with yourself, when you are without the emperor's clothing, and when you really know who you are.

That is the way to look at your business *today*, if you are to lead your business into the *future*. In order to be a leader of the *future*, your vision and values must become part of your personal fabric of today.

ACKNOWLEDGMENTS

My second grade teacher, Ms. Web, said in a report to my mother, "Troy could be Prime Minister of Australia if he only applied himself and stopped passing notes to girls in class." My technical drawing teacher in junior high pulled me aside one day and asked, "Why do you let these other idiots in the class lead you on? You are a leader, when are you going to wake up to yourself and take control? Do you really want to be like them?" I didn't listen at the time, but those messages sure do resonate now. And for the simple fact that I remember those words so far down the track, I thank you both!

Now, so many years later I reflect and think of *all* of the people who have influenced my life.

On this most recent part of our journey, I have had so many wonderful people help my beautiful wife and I with our adventures across the world, in particular, the United States. We had one wonderful guide, without whose help, would have made elements of our life a little more challenging and I would not have had the tranquility and time to write this book. My wife's Aunty Stephanie has been a gem, opening up her home, her heart, and her knowledge to help us find our footing in a new country and, in turn, finding the time for me to sit around the pool with my laptop and tap out the final chapters of this manuscript.

To my good mate and bald brother Gomez, you too have been a wonderful asset to my life and a great support for me. When I needed anything you came, without question.

To my fellow Wiley author Kevin Daum. Without you helping me construct a better manuscript and, more importantly, a better marketing strategy for the manuscript, I'd still be trying to piece the puzzle together.

Many thanks to my mother, father, and sister. And a huge thanks to my "advisory board," my inner sanctum, in particular Pete, Mick, Brad, James, John, and Tom—you have *all* lived the ride with me. Without your guidance and support, many of the stories in this book could not have been told, as so many of the positions I put myself in, I simply would not have dragged myself out of. Your words of wisdom helped guide me through. To my lifelong mates Steve and Bruce, I love coming home to Australia and having you remind me to keep it real.

And to our wonderful friends, John and Marita, thank you for the safe haven we have needed to rest and regroup in recent years. You give us the inspiration and energy to be better people and to find greater purpose to create a better future.

As a very good friend once taught me, people come into your life for a reason, a season, or a lifetime. And with each book I write, I find that I have some of each of these individuals that have contributed to the story of my journey. Thank you all for being part of my life.

INTRODUCTION

The Universal Lesson of Business

Business today is no different than business 8 years ago, 80 years ago, or 800 years ago. It has a cycle, a flow, and a transaction process that does not change. The only thing that changes is what business represents to you, and how you let that representation affect your future. People are still people, and they transact with people as they did 8, 80, or 800 years ago. They will transact the same way in another 8, 80, or 800 years from now.

Obstacles in business are simply the manifestation of your fear-based reaction to what is going on around you at that time. And each and every one of those reactions you have *today* will, in some way, impact the way you choose to handle the *future*— as you are, in fact, creating the future by the way you deal with the present.

So, before you turn the next page of this book, I want you to consider that the things you may learn will not only help you turn any current business obstacle you may have into an opportunity; they will also help you in your business when times are not so tough and even when business is great.

I have learned what I consider to be the most valuable lessons in business amidst crises, economic downturns, and potential business failures. These are the times when I have

stopped, stepped out of the business—if only for a moment—
peeled back the layers of nonsense that brought me there to
begin with, and considered what just happened to me. Then
I gave some serious thought to how I could reinvent myself
to overcome the obstacle, turn it into an opportunity, and
continue to look to the future.

Sometimes that worked. Other times, it was just a lesson
in pain I needed to learn to make me stronger for my next
challenge or business obstacle—and to keep me real.

So, whatever your situation may be, I expect that many
of the stories you read in the pages that follow will resonate
with you. And if you stop and consider what impact you can
make on your business with the information you take away
from each of these stories, then I figure you may just be on a
path to build a better, more resilient business for the future and
a more purposeful life—one that will carry you through the
tough, unusual, challenging, amazing, or uncharted times you
may be currently experiencing or may experience in years to
come.

No matter what space or place you are in right now, the
key to surviving it is to get real, get honest, and get back to the
true you.

FUTURE-PROOFING
YOUR BUSINESS

PART

I

Take Responsibility

CHAPTER

1

The Lesson of Learning

"I used to think that in order to look like a successful businessperson you needed to sound like one. Now I know that in order to sound like one you need to first be one. And there is only one way to do that: Be open and show the humility to learn from any source you can."

I started in business completely by accident. It was late 1989, and I was driving in to work at the radio station for another early start to another 16-hour day.

My life was starting to feel like the movie *Groundhog Day*; 5 A.M. start, produce the breakfast show, produce and prerecord the morning team's comedy segments for the next day's show when they came off air at 9 A.M. until about 11 A.M., go to station meetings until midafternoon, inhale some food at my studio's mixing console, pour more coffee down my throat in preparation for the second half of the day, stay locked in the darkness of the studio for another 10 hours before driving home sometime before midnight only to skull as many beers as I could in an hour before passing out on the couch, wake up at 2 A.M.

with a headache, a kink in my neck, and a dead arm and decide to go to bed—and then get up two hours later to do it all again. (Isn't the media a sexy industry?)

This had been my day for three months straight. As I drove in that morning in darkness and silence, only one sentence slipped out of my mouth into the cool air: *"This just isn't fun anymore."* I was not growing anymore; I was not going anywhere. There didn't seem to be any teachers or anything new to learn. And since the salary was terrible, there was no compensation on that front, either.

Radio had been such a great part of my life for years. I loved my time on the air in tropical North Queensland and the work-hard–play-hard approach we had. I loved my time in management. But *this* was not what I signed up for.

The station had gone through multiple owners in the course of only two years, and the most recent was the toughest. For some reason, my new program manager insisted on pushing the envelope, seemingly just for his own entertainment. He kept loading me up, and I kept taking it on in defiance. But that power play was getting old, and I realized that I'd had enough. It was time for me to start using my energy in a more positive way.

That morning, as the breakfast team came off the air and I had my first break for the day, I walked into my boss's office and announced the following: "I'm done! You've pushed me too far and for no reason. Clearly, you have someone else in mind for the job; let them have it, because I'm out." And just like that, as if a whole block of my life never happened, my radio career came to an end within hours, and I was unemployed. I got home early that night, sat and watched the sun disappear into the horizon—and the bottle of rum with it—and thought to myself, "Hmmm, okay; so, well, that's done. What next?"

So I rang one of my business mentors, real estate guru Graham Hogg, and asked his advice. We decided it would be best to put my apartment up for sale, as the market was booming and it was a good time to be selling in my particular area. It was time to cash in on the ride; so I did, and it was sold the next day.

I rang my mother and said, "I just sold my apartment . . . oh, yeah, and I quit my job on Friday." There was a silence on the line and then the inevitable question: "So, what are you going to do now?" My very confident yet poorly thought-out response: "I think I'll go buy a crappy house and renovate it, you know, see if I can cash in on the real estate boom for a little while and make some money. Wanna chip in? We'll do it together, it'll be fun!"

I thought to myself as I hung up the phone, "Okay, so not sure where that came from. But, let's have a go. What's the worst that can happen?"

And just like that, I was in business. My mother and I threw an equal amount of cash into an account, registered a business name—and then, as if it were our destiny, we were in the home renovation business with a company we named New Address.

A few weeks later, we bought a rundown, three-bedroom home in an outer city suburb. The walls looked like the previous owners had a budding graffiti artist in the family; the carpet had morphed from carpet with a bit of dog hair in it to a collection of dog hair with a hint of carpet color; the backyard appeared to be a great location for an episode of *Survivor*; the kitchen was something from a 1960s cereal commercial; and the bathroom looked like a film set for *Psycho Three: The Bathroom's Revenge*. It was perfect!

My mother did all of the interior decorating and design, and I did the deals with the real estate agents, carpenters, landscape guys, flooring guys, and any other vendor—and away we went. One house led to two, two led to three, and three to four. We fixed them and flipped them as quickly as we could, sometimes fully renovating the property in only three weeks! We stumbled from one success to the next, not learning much from each of the experiences as we completed each one, since we didn't really document any of the encounters, interactions, or events. It was all done on intuition and gut feel. We'd buy the worst house on the best street and make it look like it belonged.

I can recall one particular occasion where we settled on a property and said to the real estate agent, "Call me in four weeks; we'll be done here." After the fifth week, he pounded on the front door yelling, "You've listed the property with someone else?" I responded, "For sure! Actually, we've already sold it; we just haven't had the time to put the sign up yet. I told you ring me in four weeks, and you didn't." He explained that he didn't believe we'd really be done by then, and I just smiled as I shut the door and said, "Then maybe you better start listening to your clients. After all, I did say call me in four weeks, how quick a sale was that for him? You'd reckon the guy would have been back to me quicker that an Olympian on steroids. Nope!

I was having a blast. I'd get up at dawn, paint walls until midmorning, do some deals with vendors and agents till about lunchtime, set everyone up onsite for the afternoon and then head off to a late lunch with any of my mates who happened to have the day off. I'd get home sometime later that afternoon with a skin full of booze and continue painting into the night with many beers in hand and the stereo playing full blast. It was the perfect job; and I was perfectly oblivious to the real business implication of everything I did each day. I was simply earning more for doing less for the first time in my life—and I absolutely loved it!

That is, right up until I realized it was not a job but rather a *business* that I had; and I didn't have the first clue about how to run a business.

I was walking down the beach with a mate of mine, relaying the events of the last six months in my newfound career. I gave him the following highlights:

• We'd traded a half dozen properties.
• We had five more under contract or in the pipeline.

- It seemed like we were making close to a 20 percent margin on each of the properties. (I didn't *really* know for sure; but that felt like the amount I should be making.) Aaaannnddd our debt to equity ratio was well and truly outside of my comfort zone and climbing with each deal. That last bit got my attention. After all, until I quit my job, I had a $45,000 mortgage on a dinky two-bedroom apartment, and a broken down MG convertible that was more of a pushcart than a sports car. Every time I got it to start I'd do a victory dance! Trading that many properties in quite a short period of time after such a simple existence represented a lot of money in the late 1980s in the middle of a recession.

As soon as these words came out of my mouth, I could almost feel the shiver come over my body—and I went a little quiet. This was the first time I realized that I had *no* idea what I was doing—and that I really didn't know anything about business, or life, for that matter.

This moment of self-realization was no surprise for my friend. He was years in front of me in business and personal development and no doubt had already experienced this scary epiphany some years earlier. While he was now accustomed to making million-dollar deals every other day, this was all new for me. I was silent as we walked down the beach. The shiver left my body, and I could feel my pulse quicken a little and my brain start to buzz a bit with too many thoughts colliding all at once. Clearly, I needed to develop a better strategy for running this new business of mine—or this would all fall down like the proverbial house of cards.

I must have gone a little pale after my information download as my friend quietly asked me with a slight smirk, "You alright?" To which I responded—in my best strategic fashion—"Let's find a bar!" I figured that today it was time for me to really open up to my friend and take as much away from this conversation, and his experience, as I could.

The next few hours were good for me; they served as an early turning point in my business career. It was the first time that I think I truly *learned* anything about business. My father is a great businessman who had tried to help me understand business in the past. He had done a wonderful job of *encouraging* me to truly embrace what it meant to be in business for yourself; and if I had asked more questions or been more attentive, I surely would have learned more from him.

But this time, things were different. Now, I was *ready* to receive any information. Before today, I just figured I had to listen. I didn't have time for that business strategy stuff; I was more focused on *being* great instead of *learning how* to be great.

As I walked along the beach and reflected on my situation, I began to get angry with myself for failing to ask more questions or to listen more intently to my father almost a decade earlier. How much easier would this journey be had I done that simple thing? But I was young, proud, distracted, and a bit wet behind the ears. Now I was a decade behind where I should have been on my path to developing business smarts. Idiot!

I walked onto the beach that day as a fun-loving, self-employed bloke who thought, "How easy is this business stuff? Piece of cake—no problem!" I walked *off* the beach as a small business owner thinking, "I am dumb as dog shit. Wow—this could have ended really, *really* badly." I had clearly just received a dose of reality, and was about to learn some early lessons. It was time to get my very inexperienced head out of my very egotistical backside and actually begin to learn!

I spent the next few days grilling my friend on how he ran his business, how he planned, how he put money together so that it went in and out as it should and the cupboard was never bare. I learned how you could make money but still not *have* any money, how you could *get* money without having any money, and how you could end up without money if you did not watch the money you had closely.

It was fascinating and oh so frightening!

All of this information was so significant in that it was the first time I realized just how much responsibility I had: far more than I did as a manager and employee, even though I had run teams of up to 15 people and budgets well in excess of the property value I was trading. This new venture was totally *my* responsibility, my win—or my loss. It was time for me to stop acting like the young gun businessperson I *thought* I was and truly understand the young naive businessperson I *really* was.

And all of a sudden I was back at work full-time without a clue what I was doing or what my job really was.

I jammed as much information into my head as I could over the next few weeks. I read books, talked to people, and attended seminars—all in an effort to figure out what I should be doing and what I was currently doing wrong, or, through sheer luck, sometimes right.

Back then, I used to think that in order to look like a successful businessperson, you needed to sound like one. Now I know that in order to sound like one you need to first *be* one. And there is only one way to do that: Be open and show the humility to learn from any source you can.

And, lucky for me, that was my very first lesson.

It's been some 20 years—and 10 more companies that I have owned—since I received this brick to the head. I now know that learning does not come from a single place, person, source, or nugget of information. It is the cumulative effect of your ability to tap into all of the information you receive on a daily basis and to identify and be aware of the knowledge that each of these pieces of information offers you.

For many years, I have spoken at conferences all over the world—in 16 different countries at hundreds of engagements. And the common denominator at all of these events is that so many people in the audience are looking for the "one thing" to make life easy. They don't necessarily want to *learn*; they just want the *answer*. They're seeking a magic bullet—a key to life, the universe, and business success. They wait for the goose to arrive that will lay the proverbial golden egg. They sit at attention, pens in hand, looking up at the guy on stage.

I can almost hear their brains ticking, and I can read the same thing over and over in their eyes. "Go on, bald man; show us what you've got. Tell me how you're going to make it easy for me; give it your best shot. Impress me—give me the answers." I know that's what they're thinking, because that's what *I* thought during my early years in business as an attendee at such conferences.

They sit in silence in the audience waiting, waiting, waiting, for the explanation that will take away the hard work and make it easy for them to make a buck and lead them to success.

Well, the sad news is such a magic bullet just doesn't exist.

More important, what everyone seems to be seeking is not external. It's not something you can touch, hold, shift, or own.

It is something you feel, something you represent, something that is rooted in your core beliefs. And it starts with your ability to get back to a sense of personal reality and truth. If you can discover your most basic truth, you can break down some of the existing beliefs that are holding you back—and develop new ones that will set you on the path to a more purposeful future.

As a consultant, one thing that consistently blows me away is how totally crazy businesspeople are. They hire consultants, buy books, read magazines, subscribe to newsletters, attend conferences, study, ask questions, network, and do their genuine best to gather as much information about business as they can. (Much like you, too, are doing right now by reading this book.) But somewhere between this page and the back cover, all of the great information they have absorbed will be lost as they discard it with their fear-based business beliefs and throw it in the bin.

Why would they do that? And why would you do that?

It typically happens because you are trapped in very basic, fear-based beliefs that stop you from *really* learning. You usually come to hold these beliefs as a by-product of the unreal business environment in which we all work. Our peers, leaders, associates, and any others that have preceded us in the business world introduced them to us, and we all bought into the way *they believe* it to be. We aren't *born* with beliefs, after all; we inherit them or create them as we make our way through life. So your first challenge is to break down some of the beliefs that are bad for you.

I have honed in on four core fear-based beliefs that you need to eliminate from your thought process if you are to learn anything—and you need to do that today!

1. You don't think you have enough *time* to learn or to change anything in your life; essentially, you're too busy being busy to implement some of the lessons you've learned. You're too frazzled to stop and think; instead, you make do with what you have, and every day is Groundhog Day. You pray for every day to be easier, better, faster, more fun, more rewarding; yet, every day you fail to make the time to change anything. Then you wonder why the next day you wake up feeling the same way and launch yourself onto the same treadmill.

2. You believe that while the things you have learned and the information you have gathered may be interesting, the situation is *different* in your life, your business, your area, your country, your category. This belief prompts you to discard this information and convince yourself that any application of it in your special circumstance simply won't work for you.

3. You think that you know what you are doing, when, in actual fact, you are simply too afraid to *ask* for help. As a result, you run your business on ego rather than ability. You might not *think* you are doing that, but wouldn't you be more open to accepting some of these new lessons if you weren't?

Ego is driven by ignorance, arrogance, and fear. Ability is driven by humility, reality, and truth.

There are really only two decisions you can make in business: one is based on truth, the other on fear. If your ego does not permit you to make or admit a mistake, instead blaming others or other circumstances for your lot in life, you have chosen fear as your partner in business.

4. You *believe* you know where you are going, but you lack *vision*, and therefore purpose. So many of us get into a business without any clue about what to do next. We sometimes write extensive business plans and then fail to refer to these plans for guidance. We engage business leaders and coaches for help in the creation of a vision or plan for the business and don't bother to listen to their advice. We post things on the walls of our offices to help us visualize what we want out of life, but we don't really know *why* we want those things—other than the fact that society has implied that they represent success. Worse still, we often do not have the vision to understand when our business journey is finished. We have no idea when or where we should get off.

If purpose is your ultimate goal, then vision allows you the clarity of the future to see how you are going to achieve your goal.

Can you put your hand on your heart and sincerely tell me that you do not have *any* of those beliefs?

No, really. Stop and think about that, because if we do not get past this first challenge, then the rest of the book will merely be a nice story. And you'll finish it saying, "Yeah, *that was interesting; I can see how it worked for him. But it's different for me; I don't have the time to do any of that stuff. Besides, I'm not really sure how to make that work in my business life, and really, it's not what I want out of life, anyway. At least, I don't think so. Actually, I'm not entirely sure."*

These were the beliefs that I clung to for almost a decade—and they nearly bankrupted me. However, this was just the jolt I needed to get real, become honest, expose my real self, and take a long, hard look at my life and my actions, and prepare myself to learn.

As a young businessperson, I would run all over the world gathering information, attending conferences, and being what I thought was a human business sponge. In reality, I was talking the talk but not walking the walk. I was too afraid to implement change for fear of getting it wrong. I thought I was smart, but I was simply egotistical and arrogant. I thought I was going places, but I was simply running around in circles. I thought I was innovative, but I was just repackaging the same crappy concepts in different wrapping paper. And most of all, I thought I was a great business leader, but I was simply *threatening* everyone to follow me.

It was all wrong. And I didn't even know it.

I was making a buck, driving fast cars, living in a nice house, drinking good wine with friends—doing all the fun things that came with developing a successful private enterprise. And the reality of life was simply irrelevant to me. I was erratic, unfocused, and pretty much unaware of anything or anyone around me. I, too, was one of those small businesspeople looking for the magic bullet, searching externally for something to make success easy for me. Something "out there" of course, because surely the problem with my businesses could not be *me*!

Then came a moment of truth that forced me to get back to reality.

It was the 1990s, and I'd been in business for almost 10 years—not just one business, but a number of unrelated companies. Over the course of the previous decade, I had owned a property development business, a recording studio, an advertising and marketing business, and even a pizza shop.

Yup, a bunch of eclectic business adventures for sure. In fact, I often look back and say to myself, "Why the hell did you get into that?" The answer was that many of my professional decisions were driven by ego. I'd become involved with these businesses by convincing myself that I knew what I was doing, when all I was doing was allowing my ego to run my life and my companies. I was too afraid to ask for help and too busy telling everybody else how clever I was, for fear of bruising that ego.

I can recall a day that I was spending at home in my lounge room. We'd just bought a pizza shop and I had a bunch of mates over to celebrate. One of them remarked, "How cool is this? You get free pizza." At that moment, the reality of my business decision hit me. I looked down at the boxes of pizza strewn across the table and responded, "Free!!!! These suckers cost me $10,000 a piece!" All of a sudden, my business investment seemed ridiculous.

The simple truth was that I had a handful of businesses all running simultaneously at that time, some of them in different parts of the country, all of them doing okay and making a bit of money, but none of them doing great. In short, we lucked out on many of the decisions I was making and had stumbled to a level of moderate success. There was no ability involved, just sheer arrogance.

And then came my first moment of truth.

Almost as if interest rates went through the roof overnight, the Asian economy went through the floor. That had a severely detrimental impact on the Australian economy, and a domino effect that led to a number of our clients going out the back door.

I remember it clear as day. I was on a flight home from Tokyo, returning from yet another conference where I sat happily in the audience taking notes for days on end and gathering information and inspiration from the sensational lineup of speakers. As was normal on the journey home, my fear-based beliefs started to kick in as I went back over my notes. My self-talk was already throwing ideas out the plane window.

"Yeah, I don't have time to use that in my business. Nah, it's different for us; that won't work. Hmm . . . not sure what he meant by that, but it doesn't matter; probably won't suit us, anyway. I know what I'm doing. Yeah, I don't know why we would do that; it's not really part of our plan. I don't think so, anyway. Maybe . . . not sure."

But something snapped in me as the plane started its descent into Sydney airport. I somehow knew that this time my return home was going to be . . . well, different. I truly felt this time that I was going to make a change in my life. I just didn't know why or how. Maybe it was the profoundness of the information I had gleaned during my trip; or maybe it was just that I was *ready* for change.

As I walked up the aerobridge, I had a strange feeling. I was both excited about being home and keen to get back to work to report on some of the great things I had learned. At the same time, I was somewhat terrified that the implementation of those changes was going to be monumental!

I turned my cell phone on as I got off the plane and for the first time in four days, it kicked into the network (the Japanese cell phone network is not compatible with those of many other countries). The first call came through in the early morning chill; it was the office calling to inform me that three of our clients had announced over the weekend that they were filing for bankruptcy. My mental calculator went into overdrive and told me that little bit of news had put us in a cash hole of about $375,000.

I went out through customs at the international terminal and I got another call from one of my bankers that started out something like this: "G'day Troy. Listen, we heard about some of your clients over the weekend, and we're just giving you a call to inform you that there will be a registered letter issued to you today. We're calling up your overdraft." I protested that we were not out of terms, which was only met with, "Yeah, well, this is a precautionary move on our part, given that we know what is happening in your business at the moment with some of your clients. Since we know it will take you some time to work it out, we're just protecting our interests." Gotta love those banks; they know just how and where to put the boot when you're down. (And they wonder why nobody likes them!)

I was a bit wounded by this stage but still felt like I had a few more rounds left in me before I was going to accept a technical knockout. But shortly thereafter, I was dealt another blow from my other bank. "Yeah, G'day Troy. We're just giving you a courtesy call to let you know that you'll get some official advice in the mail in relation to your overdraft." Same story here; they wanted their money, too.

Capping this off was a call from the tax office advising me that I was about to receive a tax bill I could not jump over with a payment deadline that I could not meet.

I was taking a total and absolute belting on all fronts. And the worst part was that it was still too early in the day for a drink!

On first estimate, I figured that this was going to leave us about $500,000 in the hole by the time the tsunami had subsided; the final number climbed closer to the $1 million mark. In short, we were up the creek, and not only did we not have a paddle, we had no map and a hole in the boat to boot.

I was shattered. I had pulled many rabbits out of hats over the previous years to get us out of a poor cash position. However, I had nowhere to run this time. I don't care how solid your business is; you take that much money out of the cash flow and it ain't pretty.

I started to do some soul searching. How did I get myself into this; and how was I going to get myself *out* of this? And whose fault was it, anyway?

I got to the office and went straight to a staff meeting. I figured that the one thing I should not do was panic in front of the team. Instead, I just delivered the truth as best I could understand and describe it.

"Okay, so you've all seen the newspaper over the weekend, and you've all got a number of questions as to how we are going to get ourselves out of this spot. We've got some challenges ahead of us in the next few months, and what I want to do immediately is just make a commitment to change—one thing at a time, one day at a time—to get us back on track. And it starts *now*. Every morning we're going to have a quick staff meeting during which I am going to ask each of you three questions:

"1. How did you do yesterday?

"2. What are you focused on today?

"3. How are you going to do it better tomorrow?

"Starting today, I am focused on how we are going to protect our future. Starting tomorrow, I am going to work on being a better communicator. I am going to tell you everything that is going on in the business so you have the confidence that we'll be able to make it through this spot.

"I am going to call a meeting with each of our creditors and ask them for their support. And I am going to call a meeting with our top clients and ask that they help out, too. We've been good to them for a decade; it's time to cash in the chips. Finally, I am going to ask them to start paying for our services in advance."

The staff looked and listened, and over the course of an hour, they began to see my commitment to change.

It was one of the toughest meetings I think I have ever had, mainly because I was standing in front of my team and completely exposing myself as their leader. I was standing in my naked truth. This was the real position of the business and my honest assessment of what we needed to do to get out of the spot we were in. No sugar coating, no ego, no smoke and mirrors.

However, that was just the start of the pain. It was going to get much worse.

Early the following Saturday morning, I stood at my dining room table staring down at the pile of bills, cash flow projections, debtor and creditor printouts, and asset and liability assessments. I began to feel the enormity of the challenge ahead of us.

That morning, I called in my advisory board for an emergency meeting. We elected to engage an administrator to help us get back on our feet and—hopefully—avoid going broke. But it wasn't going to be easy. Weeks turned into months, months into years, and every day it seemed harder and harder to get out of bed. It was as if we were working so hard and so quickly to repair the damage, and yet everything seemed to be moving so slowly. I felt like Steve Austin in one of those running scenes from the *Six Million Dollar Man*. I knew I could go fast, but it just didn't look that way to others.

My marriage took a hammering. I was working back-to-back 16-hour days in an out-of–shape, overweight body. Each day morphed into the next, and I seemed to only get a break from the beating when I crawled home and inhaled as many beers as I could before passing out for a few hours—only to get up and do it all over again.

I was in a very bad place.

But, pain and heartache aside, one of the greatest things I learned through this period was that if I was to get back on track,

---

I had to once again face the truth and address the one common denominator between success and failure in any of my businesses or my life. It was me!

Some 10 years earlier on the beach I had learned my first lesson, the lesson of learning. Well, it seemed it was time for me to remind myself how to start really learning again.

It was time for me to start looking *internally* instead of externally for the solution to my problems.

And it occurred to me that learning how to learn is not something you do once. It is something you need to continually remind yourself to do, or you will inevitably return to poor belief systems. It is a continual journey, and not just one that's focused on business; it requires that we go back to a sense of self and a place of truth and reality. This was a perspective I had lost over the previous 10 years, so I needed to relearn some of the things I had forgotten. And not just about business, but things about *me*. I needed to peel back some of the layers of unreality that had yet again become part of my being and learn to be comfortable in my skin once more.

I realized how simple it was for a career-centric mind to become trapped in the wrong beliefs, even when we know, on some level, that they're wrong. I began to see how easy it is for businesspeople to get so caught up in the professional tornado that they also lose a sense of being and forget what they are really trying to achieve among the noise.

So, before we get into the questions you really want answered, let me share my first lesson: the lesson of learning.

Now, I want you to work with me here for a moment. I need you to clear your mind totally to be able to effectively receive the information on the following pages. I need you to go back to basics, set aside some of those fear-based beliefs, and get true to you.

Let's make a start.

You'll notice throughout this book that I will give you little exercises to do, things to try, or notions to ponder at a later date—thought-starters, if you will. They are designed to help you form snapshots of what you look like now and what you *could* look like in the future if you put your mind to it. But before we get into conquering your fear-based beliefs and preparing you for change in business, I want you to do the following for me.

Grab a pad, a journal, or use the workbook note pages in the back of this book—anything you can use to keep notes on the things you may learn. This is a place for you to reflect when you've finished each chapter and gathered the information. This is *important*. If you don't record the information, the messages I am about to deliver to you in my stories will get jumbled and will be open to all sorts of strange interpretation. And then they'll inevitably get caught up in your old, fear-based beliefs, and the unreality of your life will kick back in and stop you from learning.

Let me offer you a scenario of your business and life right here, right now.

You have about a million business decisions to make right now. Your head is muddled with stuff. You wake up most days tired from the day before and the lack of sleep you've had overnight from thinking about what you need to deal with today. I call it "the rattles"—the 3 A.M. toss and turn as you try and piece one business day together with the next and the decisions you have to make in an effort to find some flow. You feel like you are pushing square pegs in round holes and it's just, well, *hard*. I know how this feels. I lived it for almost two decades.

Remember how fun it was when you started out in business? You had a blank slate, no preconceived ideas on how everything should work; you just made it up as you went along and seized opportunities as they were presented to you. And each morning you jumped out of bed to get into the day, and you loved it!

So what changed?

You did.

Business didn't all of a sudden get tougher somehow; you just started to put more boundaries on it. Customers did not all abruptly become hard work; you just lost interest in working with them. Your staff did not suddenly become incompetent oxygen thieves with the IQ of a small, stuffed parrot; you just stopped leading and training them, and you lost interest in their lives. And though the economy *did* change, it didn't happen overnight; you were just not on top of the numbers as tightly as you should have been in the good times to prepare for the inevitable economic cycle and the bad times that come with that.

Economic change is indeed an interesting phenomenon. As soon as we experience a bump in the road, it rapidly turns into a minor road hazard, then into a pothole, then a major roadblock. And then everybody stands around looking at it, wondering who should fix it, while trying to figure out who *else* they can hand the shovel to. It's a bit like the council, really.

The fact is that every economic correction simply signals the end of the cycle. Think about it; the banks irresponsibly lent money to a lot of people who quite possibly were not able to pay it back. These people took that money irresponsibly, knowing, at least in part, that they were going to struggle to pay it back should something shift in the market. Businesses oversold to those people and took some of that newfound, negligently attained wealth so that they, too, could cash in on the gravy train. They then immediately went out and spent that money recklessly, while ignoring the likelihood that there would no doubt be another shift in the market sometime; after all, this has historically been the case. And the government sat around and watched this happen—for years! And their excuse for their inaction was to take the accolades that they were, in fact, "growing the economy as part of the economic development strategy". . . yeah right! Just a bunch of political, economic handbags on both sides of the fence.

And then, seemingly out of the blue—as if by total accident—the bubble burst, and everyone stood around asking, "Wow, how did *that* happen?" Well guess what? It happens every 7 to 10 years; it has been happening since the Great Depression, and it will happen again sometime in the future. Boom, boom, boom, bust, recovery. It's a cycle!

So who is responsible for all that? *We all are!*

It took me three major economic shifts to figure that out. The first one I experienced as a businessperson was during the 1980s, and it cost me $250,000. The second took place in the 1990s, and cost me closer to $1 million. My third experience came in the early 2000s with the tech wreck or dot-com bust. By this time, however, I had become a little smarter, and bought into technology *after* the bubble burst in 2001. Then, coming into 2007, my colleagues and I began to see the signs once again, so we contained debt and battened down the hatches as best we could in preparation for the inevitable crash. And *still* I found myself not as ready as I wanted to be. I can look back now and see strategies that would have better prepared us for the end of the cycle; these are all things we can do next time to ensure that we are more resilient.

So, what am I trying to say with all of this? It's a tough thing to look at that mirror, however, at the end of the day, *you* are the common denominator between success and failure in business and in life. It's all about you!

Unless you get yourself on track, there is no way in the world that you can get your business on track. So let's start there. Let's get you back to your truth and rebuild the new you in preparation to learn, *before* we look to rebuild your business.

I didn't write this book as a way to sympathize with you or admit that it really *is* too hard. I am not here to say, "There, there, I understand; it will all be alright. Just attract better things into your life, and everything will fall into place." This is not about us all having a group pity party and a good whine about how the banks/government/business leaders/economists/ (insert anything you like here) got it wrong. This *is* about saying, "Screw them; *I* need to take responsibility, get real, and fix this myself." This is about getting off your backside to make that change, to tackle the really hard things in your life head-on and drag yourself out of Groundhog Day and into a new way of life that maybe—just maybe—might not be so hard!

After all, hard is just a perception.

You see, as humans, we forget "easy," and in fact, we *create* hard. The world in which we live constantly sends us messages about things to learn, do, be, and aspire to. Yet the most "real" most of us ever were was during our early years on this planet, when we had little exposure to the world. Back then, we were free from the corruption of perception and were truly living in reality.

And that's where I want to get you back to—your reality and your truth. Because only then can you face the real issues in your life and truly make it easier than it is right now.

Okay, now that you know you are going to have to face some tough issues in your life, here's the second bit of unpleasant news. In the search for easy, I know you'll be looking for simple answers, quick fixes, and overnight solutions. You're probably thinking, "Just tell me what to do and I'll be on my way to ease, happiness, and contentment." Well, I'm not here to give you that gem, either. I'm just here to offer you some of the life and business lessons that I, and others, have learned so that you might find easy yourself.

The journey is long, but if we are to truly plan a stronger future for ourselves, then we need to be clear that every action we take *today* will have a reaction on the future of our business and our lives *tomorrow*.

Let's start by clearing your head and taking responsibility for learning.

Taking Responsibility to Learn

Three things you need to do now to Future-Proof Your Business and prepare yourself to truly learn

Action One

Put your hand on your heart—right here and now—and ask yourself: "Am I really in my truth? Do I genuinely believe that I am making my decisions based on truth, not fear? Am I caught in any of the four killer belief systems that will stop me from absorbing information and, in turn, ultimately cause me to get in my own way on my path to success?"

(continued)

(*Continued*)

Ask yourself this question *every single day*. Make it a habit. Don't take the easy, fear-induced road when faced with a tough decision; take the one that leads to truth and reality. When gathering information for your business, make sure you are not succumbing to any of the four killer fear-based beliefs before you discard it.

Action Two

Know the *real* position of your business, not the safe position you have sold to yourself. Write that down, stare at it, absorb it, own it, take responsibility, and deal with it. Don't cut corners on your reporting and accountability to yourself.

You can only really apply the things you learn in life if you are applying them to the honest position you're currently in. Lying to yourself will only come back and bite you five times harder somewhere down the track. However, building on a platform of reality will, in turn, offer you a *real* outcome.

Action Three

Ask yourself every time you receive any piece of information, "Am I really, truly open to learning and absorbing things around me?" Are you ready to make a commitment to becoming more aware?

That's you being true, being real, and down to business. And that's your first step to becoming a success.

CHAPTER

2

Truth and Reality versus Fear and Greed

"The further you wander from your truth in business, the further you wander from your purpose and, in turn, your path to success. Call it karma if you will, what goes around comes around."

How do you reckon you rate when it comes to being true to yourself? Do you really put your hand on your heart each morning and say, "Today, I am only going to deal in reality and truth. I am not going to lie to myself. And I am not going to be afraid."

It sounds pretty easy, doesn't it?

But the fact is each and every day we are faced with the option to make choices based on truth or fear. And every time I make a major decision in life based on fear, I end up in a world of hurt somewhere down the line. My biggest problem was that I would never work that out until a point in the

25

future when it was too late. In fact, even after years of working in private enterprise and consulting to businesses all over the world, I've learned that the cause behind most of the issues that businesspeople experience is their failure to deal in reality or truth in the present, and this impacts significantly on their future. People will cover things up, blame others or certain circumstances, and hide behind problems in an effort to avoid facing the truth. Often, the truth is related to their actions—or lack thereof—on a particular issue.

I first became aware of this tendency on my part during the 1990s. I was developing my businesses faster than Clark Kent could change undies in a phone booth, and my core focus was growth. I was not after just ordinary growth, I wanted it *fast*. You see, I had to keep up with my mates. I was surrounded by successful entrepreneurs, all of whom were out to make the "Rich List" before their 40th birthdays. And I got sucked into the ride.

We took on clients left and right who only had to meet one criterion: pass our pulse check. In other words, they had to have a pulse and a check. As a result, I often found myself in my boardroom giving presentations to potential clients thinking to myself, "I don't even like this guy. He seems too smooth, and he comes across like he's light on business ethics and integrity. And I'm not really excited about the project either; I don't think it's got legs."

And yet, despite my gut reactions, I'd take on the clients, just for the money and the growth—a total fear-based decision. I was afraid that if I didn't make the deal or take the business, then I wouldn't make budget and, in turn, would not make the "fastest growing companies list" or some other pathetic, egotistical, fear-based measure of success.

Of course, every time we did this, the business relationship would end in tears. The client would complain about something ridiculous and refuse to pay his bills. We'd be frustrated with the client's lack of professionalism and waste countless hours of our time executing projects that should have gone smoothly but didn't, or that we never got paid for.

The *truth* is, I should have followed my intuition and said, "No thanks; I don't think we can do business together," and walked away from the deal. The *reality* was that I acted based on my fear that if I did not take on the client, we would not grow.

It took me years to realize that we simply did not make money from clients who we did not trust nor respect, or with whom we did not get along—no matter who they were or how big the project.

I came to the point where—upon analyzing our six-million-dollar client base—I figured out that over 60 percent of those clients were not profitable. Interestingly, it was the same 60 percent of the clients that we didn't like, respect, or trust.

In short, 60 percent of our clients *sucked*!

I sat down and started to look more closely at where the money *was* coming from, and confirmed that in fact, two-thirds of our revenue was coming from new clients, with the remaining third coming from clients with whom we'd been working for over two years.

Upon further analysis, I came to see this new business as time consuming and labor intense, since it took time for us to get our new partners accustomed to the way we worked. As a result, these clients showed much less profit in the jobs we were doing for them, and they were also a lot less loyal. We seemed to be constantly forced to prove ourselves to them to keep their business, only to then have to wait for our money, which never seemed to arrive on time, either.

So I split the client list into two groups.

1. Clients who paid on time, saw the value of our service, and had been loyal to us over a period of time.
2. Clients who were slow to pay and wasted our time with their constant and usually ridiculous demands.

I woke up on New Year's Day in 2000 and sent a note to my entire staff that said: "Beginning now, our new criteria for taking on new business will be that we like the client and that they are prepared to pay our price. Do not deviate from this and follow your intuition, and don't try to make any potential clients fit into our culture, people, and what we stand for."

Then I sat down and wrote a letter to each and every client in group two on the "60 Percent Suck List" that simply said: "Thanks for being an important client of ours. Unfortunately, our business model has recently changed, and we can no longer work for you. We will do our best to place you with another firm should you require some assistance." And just like that, more than half of our clients were gone.

The staff's response was overwhelming. Morale shot up 1,000 percent; all of a sudden, we were making money on every project. It was amazing. I found myself walking out of meetings saying, "I like them, let's work with them," or "I don't like the way they think, let's pass on this one." Either way, I was happy.

We were finally living in truth when it came to new client selection. When potential clients asked us why they should hire us, I found myself repeating the same words that I had used to explain the situation to my staff: 'Because you like us, and you are prepared to pay our price, on our terms.'

In essence, because we were taking a longer look at our potential clients before bringing them on board, it forced us to look into the future relationship we were likely to have with them if they indeed did become one of our clients. We often found ourselves sitting around a table hypothesizing how the client relationship would unfold. Would they be a fit? How did we see the business growing with them, or them with us? Did their values and vision match ours? And every time we answered the questions we became more comfortable with our decisions.

And our terms changed as well, as we started to take a 50 percent payment up front. I figured that if both parties were being honest about wanting to do business together, then as a sign of good faith we'd start the work if they paid part of the bill up front. And wouldn't you know it—that worked as well. Not a single client bucked—because we had developed an open and honest relationship.

The by-product of this whole event was that by admitting to the staff that 60 percent of our client base had sucked, I was also admitting that I was the one who had brought in bad business and made their lives hell in the process. That alone earned me more respect from them in one week than I had gained in almost a decade.

I could name a dozen other times like this when things had gone pear-shaped (to use a bit of Australian slang) or gone awry in the business as a result of my not acting in truth and falling victim to fear-based decisions.

Fear is mainly driven by arrogance and ego. And arrogant businesspeople usually don't just make decisions based on fear; as leaders, they also rule by fear. This is frequently due to the fact that they doubt their true ability or worry that they will be found out or uncovered as dishonest or fraudulent. On the other hand, confident businesspeople are in touch with their reality and typically take responsibility for their actions. They claim their position, in life, and in business instead of blaming others for it.

The further you wander from your truth in business, the further you wander from your purpose—and eventually, your path to success. Call it karma if you will, but what goes around usually comes around. Your dishonesty and lies—in particular, the ones you tell yourself—will usually come back to bite you in a time and place when you least expect it.

Here are some quick tips to keep you on the straight and narrow and in touch with your reality and truth. I like to call this my little "Truth Test."

Is it perception or reality? Are you dealing with the real issue at hand or just the perceived issue on the surface?

Dig a little deeper; there might be more to your situation than you realize, and the real issue might just come back to your own actions.

Claim, not blame. Claim responsibility for *everything*. It is your life and your business, after all; you are responsible for its success or failure. So take control. If you do make a mistake, put your hand on your heart and say, "Yup, I screwed up—and here's how I am going to fix it." Confident leaders admit mistakes and believe that they can remedy them. They focus on the solution, not the problem.

Share issues with staff; if they can *see* it they can help *solve* it. Let your staff know about any issues you're facing and the reality of the situations at hand. After all, they can only help you solve them if they know these situations exist.

Listen to yourself first, then listen to others. It's easy to find the experts around you; they're the first ones to tell you that *they* know better. You know who I'm talking about: the people who start their sentences with phrases like, "You should . . .," "Why don't you . . .," or "How come you haven't . . .?" You know when you are not in touch with your truth, so stop and listen to your intuition talking to *you* first.

Truth or fear? Before you make that key decision or take any significant action, ask yourself this simple question: Are you making the decision based on truth or fear?

That last part of the Truth Test is the big one. Often, when I ask that question of others, they will inquire, "How can I tell if I am making a fear-based action or decision?" It's not that hard if you stop and think about the *real* reason why you are doing something.

You see, the truth does not hurt us; it's our *resistance* to the truth that hurts.

Don't get me wrong; this is not as easy as it sounds. Some of your decisions will be tough, and some will be life-changing. Others will be somewhat complex, and have long-ranging impact on your business and on your life.

Whenever you are in doubt as to whether you are working with truth and reality, try doing the following: Stop for a moment and clear your mind. Stop trying to figure it out, and start trying to *feel* it out. Think of the first emotion that entered your body in relation to the issue you are dealing with, and how that affected you in that instant. Remember that feeling. And then go through your little Truth Test with your hand on your heart and answer the questions as honestly as you can.

Your body will actually tell you if you are lying to yourself. That little ping in the bottom of your stomach will give it away. It's like the one you used to get when you lied to your parents about taking the last cookie, or smoking behind the school fence, or the $20 you nicked from their wallet to give to your tallest school mate so he could buy you the beer you shouldn't have been buying from the liquor store.

You know the feeling. And if that's what you feel about your decision or action, then get back to your reality and run through the Truth Test again.

If, however, you feel lightness, freeness, and a sense of ease, then you are acting in truth and reality. Go with the flow.

Use this as your daily mantra before you head into the office.

"Today I am not going to lie—especially not to myself. I am going to look at myself in the mirror, claim responsibility for all my actions, and not blame others or other circumstances. I am only going to deal with the real issues in my life."

Now that I have prepared you for your learning adventure by clearing your mind and getting you a bit closer to your truth, we're ready to go a little deeper.

Taking Responsibility to Face Your Fear and Act in Truth!

Three things you need to do now to Future-Proof Your Business and ensure that you are acting in truth—not fear.

Action One

When faced with a decision, run it past your Truth Test—and don't cut corners on your answers. Take notice of your feelings as you do that. Are you light, free, and at ease? Or do you have a knot in the bottom of your stomach or a chill through your body?

Action Two

Share the truth with those who are there to support you—your family, staff, and peers. Take a note of how often you explain your situation to them. Are you "telling it" or "selling it"? If you have to sell it then take a closer look at the reality of the information you are distributing.

Action Three

Always, always, *always* claim not blame.

CHAPTER

3

Make Time to Make It Easier

"I've had a few times in my business life when I have simply hit the wall. For me, the key was to get back to a place where I was going with the flow, and simply letting go."

I remember it like it was yesterday. It was December 28, 2006—a moment in life where I knew I had hit that wall. *Again!* But it was much worse this time. This made any difficulty I had previously encountered in business or in life look like a scene from a *Wiggles* movie.

I had just been through one of the best but toughest years of my life—personally, professionally, and psychologically. I had been on the road for 246 days, taken over 100 plane flights, circumnavigated the world 5 times, delivered more than 100 conference presentations, and lifted our combined group company profit for the year by 36 percent. I had hosted a national business TV show and served as global president of a leading entrepreneurial organization. And to top things off, along the way, I managed to have two personal relationships in my life crash and burn.

I lived in houses with water views, drove expensive cars, raced cars on weekends, flew first class, stayed all over the world in penthouse suites, and went to long lunches.

Yet, it was all wrong.

Actually, no. *It* wasn't wrong; *I* was all wrong. I just did not know it. I mean, think about it. How could one person be doing all that and *still* say that life is just too hard? After all, didn't I have the things that everyone aspires to have and be? Don't we all want big houses, fast cars, and first-class travel? That's what it's all about—right? That's what the DVDs and the books and some of the world's great speakers tell us we should be seeking. That's what makes it "easy."

That's what makes your life okay, right?

Wrong!

I *had* managed to attract these things; they just didn't make life any easier or allow me to live in my truth or in a real world. And along the way, I had also attracted a lot of clutter in my head that was also making it hard for me to distinguish what was real from what was not. Everything just got faster and faster and faster until BANG—it turned into a tornado.

Over a period of some 15 years, I had lost control of my life as a result of trying to control it *too* much. It was not mine at all; it belonged to a person I had manufactured to be me over the years as I numbed my circumstances and the world around me. I was taking no notice of what I was doing, how I was doing it, or how I was feeling. I was a shell of a man and just did not know it. Nor did so many of those around me; they, too, were living this same kind of life and were completely unaware of what was happening to them as well.

On that morning of December 28, I had absolutely *no* brain space left. I felt like everything about which I had to make a decision was hard—even the simple things.

Everything seemed like an arduous task.

I've come to realize that this feeling typically comes about when I am trying too hard to *figure* stuff out instead of feeling it out. It happens when you find yourself pushing square pegs into round holes as you fight the system and find your belief systems conflicting with reality. The key for me was to return to a place where I was going with the flow and simply finding a way of letting go.

That's what tends to happen in life. Somewhere along your journey, you get sucked up into the business tornado. You're dragged into the eye of the storm and you don't even know it until it spits you out and throws you to the ground at warp speed. It's like what happens when you throw a frog into a pot of boiling water—it jumps out. Put it into a pot of cold water, however, and slowly turn up the heat, and it will adapt to the environment without noticing until it boils to death.

That's how the tornado sucks you in without your awareness—and that's what had happened to me. At the time, I simply didn't realize the environment around me was killing me.

In the three months that followed that December morning, I took time off to reconstruct my life and attempt to figure out what had happened to me as I had become a stranger to myself. It was a time for me to regroup and identify what was *really* important in my life—and to truly understand how to avoid getting myself into that position again.

Step one for me was to let go.

I had to abandon all of the beliefs I had created in recent years and start again. One of the most powerful things I learnt was that the *definition* of success is very personal. I had to quit continually trying to be a success in others' eyes in favor of simply creating my own success in life. And I had to let go of the deep-seated desire to influence *every* outcome in life and instead simply let life in.

Now, I am sure that sounds to some of you like I sat on a hill and talked to nature for a few months. In reality, all I did was relinquish some control over my life. I began to actively look for ways to open myself up to the world again and be *aware* of what was happening around me, such that I might let it influence me more positively on my journey. And a key to allowing that to happen was to make time to let these thoughts into my day.

As I pondered life for those weeks, I quickly realized that something was placed in front of me every day that could well be a positive influence on my life—if I just let it. I simply needed to find a way to clear my head and let new thoughts in. I needed to declutter my mind.

For me, that meant making a conscious decision to find 30 minutes every day to *invite* change into my life.

Sounds pretty easy, doesn't it? However, this is the very thing that can become an Achilles' heel to the average businessperson.

Pretend you have never been in business before; in fact, imagine that you've only just arrived on this planet. You have no preconceived thoughts, no conditioning, no belief system, no barriers to any information you may receive. Pull out a blank piece of paper and write the date and the following at the top of the page: "I give up. I can't fix *everything*, and I am not going to keep pushing. I have influenced as much as I can, and I'm just going to let life happen around me and present solutions as they are meant to happen. I am just going to let it go!"

"That's got to be the most ridiculous thing I've ever heard," I can hear you saying. "Are you on crack? What the hell are you thinking? I'm in business. I can't do that; I'll go broke! What do you mean, don't make a decision—let go of control of these things? What total crap! That will never work!"

Well, if you don't trust in *me*, then trust in *yourself*.

This is not about ceasing to make decisions and failing to take responsibility for your business or your life. In fact, it's quite the contrary. This is simply about cleaning out your life and getting rid of the jumble. You likely do it all the time with your desk, so why not do the same with your mind?

That's precisely what I'd like you to do now. Get out your paper, and let's make a start at decluttering and letting go. Let's help you purge some useless information from your brain and make some space for you to absorb change.

Here's a small sample of one of mine from some time back.

Brain Dump

Things I Can Influence Today

The new speaking topics I am working on

New marketing materials for the New Year

Public relations for the New Year

Cash flow

Things I Have Influenced Enough and Need to Set Aside

My business strategy for the next 12 months

New clients in the New Year

When I will finish my next book

Things I Can No Longer Influence nor Will Allow to Take up Space in My Mind

My family's and friends' assessment of my life

Those who have let me down in business in the last 12 months

Poor past business investments

Now I make it a ritual to take time out every day to separate my thoughts into those three brain silos and to write thoughts of the future in my journal. I write the date at the top and then unload all of the information and decisions that I cannot act upon or change and do a brain dump to unclutter my mind. The secret to making this work is to be *honest* about the issues you're facing right now. Be completely candid about what you are feeling and get back to figuring out what your business and life *truly* look like.

By doing your brain dump you might un-clutter your brain enough to be able to look at an old issue in a new light, with the extra headspace.

And that is a wonderful thought to leave you on for this chapter—and a great segue to my next lesson on how to *Future-Proof Your Business*.

Taking Responsibility to Make Time!

Three things you need to do now to Future-Proof Your Business, get comfortable in your skin, and let go.

Action One

How much clutter do you have in your life? How many times have you said, "I had a feeling that would happen," but didn't act on it? How many times have you woken up tired before you even started the day? These are all signs of not going with the flow of life. You continuously attempt to push square pegs in round holes.

To open yourself to the signs that are presented to you in life—and to be aware of the *synchronicity* that life deals you and the things that come past you every day—you need to create space in that jumbled mind of yours.

Do your brain dump daily.

- Write down the things that you *can* influence today.
- Write down the things you *have* influenced enough and need to set aside.

- Write down the things that you can no longer influence and do not need taking up space in your mind.

Action Two

Question *everything*. Everything you're given and faced with is there for a reason. Open up your mind daily to the things that are happening around you. Let go, and let these things into your life rather than shutting them out with your belief systems. They may well be there to make your life easier.

By questioning everything, you in turn look more deeply at the potential opportunity that has been placed in front of you.

Action Three

Wake up every day and repeat these words: I am going to let go and go with the flow.

Review You

The Value of Vision

"You need to know where you are going and why you are going there well before you try and work out where your business is going and why."

Do you remember the question you were constantly asked coming through school: "What do you want to be when you grow up?" Do you remember some of your answers? Did you have any idea back then, or were you very clear on your future? Do you sometimes look back and laugh at what you thought you might become?

It's tough for many of us to know how to answer that question at such a young age. I can remember telling my careers advisor that I wanted to be a motor mechanic and a race car driver. However, age and clarity have taught me that I have no interest in fixing anything mechanical. In fact, I don't even own any tools. I can only recall popping the hood of my car twice ... both times by accident. And while I do love getting the race car out onto the track, I suck as a driver. I mean, I love it, and I'd do it every day of my life if I could, but I am surprised that my fellow race drivers have not changed the name on the side of the car from Hazard to something like Magoo. Hazard just sounds way too fast.

I was 36 years old before I could answer that question and 44 before I could solidify my answer into a real purpose. My career up to those points in my life was so incredibly diverse that there was *no way* I could have picked a correct answer when I was 16.

In fact, looking back on my business career's many twists and turns just makes me feel tired. I went from shop assistant, to fishing tackle salesperson, to radio announcer, to television production guy, to property developer, then recording studio owner, to advertising guy, then from business consultant, to pizza shop owner, to technology company owner, and finally public speaker and author. And those are just the highlights. Most people have had fewer jobs than I have had businesses. Madonna's *wardrobe* has less diversity than my career!

As was the case with me for much of my business career, most businesspeople still can't answer the question, "What do you want to be when you grow up?" Every day that I speak at a conference and look into the crowd of participants, I see so many lost souls. They get up, go to work, do their jobs, count the money (or lack thereof), shut up shop, and head home. If they are lucky enough to get home early enough, they play with the kids, eat, sleep—and get up and do it again.

I did the same for so many years.

The turning point for me came during a simple sales meeting in the 1990s. As usual, I had called my entire team into the boardroom to talk about our strategic plan for the next quarter. In other words, I just needed to tell them the new sales budgets. My internal strategy was simply to sell more stuff as quickly as possible, because we needed the money to fuel our ever-growing beast. My external strategy and message to the team was a little more positive and upbeat. Our previous target had been $6 million in billings, and I was standing before them all as the consummate leader, pumping up the team and slapping my hand on the table in full motivation mode proclaiming, "We've done so well, but our next target should be $6.5 million—and I reckon we can do it!"

You've heard it before; it's the "go team go" speech that coaches all over the world love to give as they high-five those around them, yell "yeah" and "right on" for no apparent reason, and punch the air like Tom Cruise on *Oprah*. Yup, that was me . . . right up until the moment a simple question was posed to me.

From the back of the room, one of my young salespeople put up his hand as I was midsentence. He dutifully waited for me to pause and said, "I think I understand, Troy, but I am curious; why $6.5 million? I don't mean to sound like I am being smart or disrespectful, I'd just like to know why *that* number and not some other number. And why do you reckon we need to do that? I mean, what is your *vision* for the company—where are we taking it, what do you think our future looks like? And I'd like to know where *you* want to be in 10 years time. That'd help me plan *my* future."

It was the kind of "movie moment" where the camera zooms in from a wide shot at the back of the room to an extreme close up of the star's face as he looks intently at nothing.

You could almost hear crickets in the silence.

I stared at him and then out the window for what seemed like 20 minutes. The world had gone into slow motion, and in a nanosecond I was moving at a tenth of time. In reality, it was probably only about five seconds or so, but because I didn't really have an answer, time dragged as all eyes were watching me, waiting for one. Everyone was sitting forward, ears straining, listening for the next sounds and the next piece of gold to come out of my mouth.

And I had *nothin'*!

Instead, I launched into a completely meaningless monologue, going on about how "If we were not growing the business, we were going backward," and "If we do not keep up with our opposition, we'll get crushed in the rush," and "We need the cash flow to fund new business and equipment to stay on our game." The whole time I was thinking in the back of my head, my God, I sound like one of those cheap-suited motivational speakers on video that I used to hate watching years ago.

I was almost waiting for myself to say something along the lines of, "Come on! Let's do this together as a team, because *together everyone achieves more!*" Fortunately, that gem did not fall out of my mouth. I did manage to save *some* dignity by leaving just one cliché out of my verbal diarrhea.

To this day, I'm still not sure how they took it, but I do know I was making *myself* sick!

About 15 minutes later, my entire team stood and left the room in silence. I closed the door after them and turned around to sit and stare out the window. *Wow*, that was a wake-up call. I replayed the event in my head over and over and over; and it got worse every time. With each hit of the rewind button, the reality of my stupidity would punch me in the bottom of my stomach and form a knot.

I figured out that after that little moment I was not *leading* my team by any means; I was *threatening* them to follow me.

What had I come up with? Well, a few things:

- Fear-based leadership is rooted in ego. The phrases I was using—"if we don't do this," "we have to," "you need to"—contained all the wrong words!
- I could no longer pretend that I had any notion of a "vision"; my team was well aware that I not only had no idea of where we were going but also that I had no clue as to how the hell I could lead them there. They were looking to me for a destination, or at least a path for the journey, and I had neither. My ego was telling me that I needed more, more, more; but I honestly couldn't figure out why.

I sat with this realization for a few weeks and tried to figure out how I could come up with this vision.

One thing I *did not* want to do was dream up one of those stupid statements that get pinned up on office walls. You've seen them, I'm sure; they're the ones that nobody reads and nobody cares about. It's the sentence that companies all over the world pay ridiculous amounts of money for consultants to create, and after 20 focus groups, 200 staff interviews, 6 months, and $50,000, they usually end up with something like:

"Our vision is to grow the company to become a leader in its field by exceeding customer expectations and offering our staff purpose and clarity in their work . . . blah blah blah—*whatever!*"

On day one, the sign goes up on the wall, and the CEO stands back like a proud, new father gazing at his baby girl through the glass in the hospital nursery. You polish the sign, you make sure it's well-lit, and you feel "complete."

On day two, you walk past with a smile, confident that it will change the world. After week one, you glance at it, still feeling some amount of pride but nervous that you are not really feeling a change in the business. Month one passes and you don't even notice the sign as you pass. After the second month, you do notice that something is not quite right with your shiny, new vision statement sign. You pause and look at it only to notice that the staff has drawn little smiley faces in the Os. A few months later, the sign comes down, and you start the process all over again as you announce to the team "We need to get back to our core values and create a stronger vision for the business."

And the cycle continues.

It was at about this same time that I attended a conference and found myself in a bar with a mate of mine from New York. He'd done very well in recent years growing his company from a standing start and taking it to IPO in only a few short years. Given my current dilemma, I figured this was a great opportunity for me to get some fantastic information from him over a beer (or 20). So I asked the obvious question: "How did you work out what your vision was, and how much of an impact did that have on the growth and success of your business?" He launched back at me like I had just called his grandmother a crack whore and barked, "Our vision had *everything* to do with our growth and success!" And over the course of the next four hours, he gave me some valuable insight as to how he runs his business based on a very clear and concise personal vision. He also explained to me that his business vision links directly to his personal vision of what he wanted to be "when he grew up."

I went back over all of this information on the way home on the plane. I thought to myself, hmmm, lots of good things to learn there. However, I realized that I needed to put it into the proper format if I was to reflect on it and make it mean something—and not be just another frame on the wall. I needed to find a way to continually review where I was going if I was ever going to lead myself purposefully into the future.

If, as individuals, we don't know what we want to be when we grow up, then we have absolutely no chance of being able to lead others to a similar place for themselves.

Once we're able to figure this out, then we first need to share that with our closest supporters—our family and friends. Then we can determine how the business is relevant to that vision as the financial driver to help us make a quid to pay for all the things you see in your vision. And then we can decide how we are going to dial in our staff to help drive that position in the business. Sounds simple, huh?

I spent hours on the plane ride home writing, looking for a simple path to pull these thoughts together. I kept repeating the conversation in the bar over and over in my head, trying to rework the details to form some kind of a path. But the solution needed to be simple if this was going to work for me. It was going to take me some time to figure this out—and even longer for me to get it right. But, I at least made a start on that plane ride home. And this is what I came up with to help facilitate that thought process:

I broke my vision down into four parts, each of which drove the other to fulfill its individual mission, and ultimately, the overall vision. This way, all roads led to what I wanted to be when I grew up.

Part 1 of the Vision

My Personal Plan

- What do I want to be when I grow up?
- What is really important to me?
- What do I want to represent?
- What are my values?
- What is my true purpose?
- How do I propose to fulfill these things?

While these questions were difficult for me, I knew they needed to be answered if I was to find my way. And to make it even harder, I knew that they were all linked—no matter how much I tried to separate them. I also knew that I needed to answer these questions first if I was to be able to create *any* vision in my life.

Since I'd already had so many wonderful and interesting life and business experiences, I found it difficult to work out what's next, what was important, or even what was real anymore. But I knew I had to solve this quandary if I was to keep focused and give myself some reason to get out of bed each day.

Money was not even close to being the right answer. I knew that no matter what, I was not going to starve nor be unable to provide for those who needed me, such as family and friends. And I had enough to do what I wanted to do personally.

My motivation needed to be more than just stuff.

Countless questions were running through my head: What was I good at? What made me the happiest? What did I want to leave behind when I was gone? What would I want someone to write on my headstone when I was dead?

And I came up with one word:

Love.

I was most content when I felt love, when I was *in* love. I was most content when I was doing something I loved and felt entirely fulfilled when I could feel the love I generated in others—the love for what they were doing in their lives.

I sat on the plane and stared out at the water below me and thought to myself, "Oh man—how soft is *that?* Where did that come from?" I was still pondering that question as my next gin and tonic arrived at my seat . . . hmmmm . . .

So where did that *love* come from? I learned years later that it came from a place of truth.

Think about it. It's rare for you to say that you love something when you truthfully hate it. It doesn't matter if it's a person, object, or action. If you are trying to convince yourself that you love something you don't, your body will reveal your true feelings. If it actually makes you unhappy, you'll feel some resistance to the truth.

I sat with that for much of the trip home and thought, "Hmmm, maybe I'm onto something." Since it was so *not* a traditionally logical business thought, I thought it might just be the breakthrough I needed to get past the unreality and superficial nature of business—and what that can do to a person.

So, as a practice run, I started to write down all of the things I loved or loved doing, in no particular order. Here's a small sample:

In Life

- Spending time with my family and friends.
- Learning and growing.

- Being by the water.
- Traveling and learning about new places and people.
- Motor sport and the rush of racing my car.
- The belief and respect that comes from the true love of a partner.
- The thought of a family of my own.
- Meeting new people that become part of my journey.

In Business

- Speaking on stage and sharing stories so that others may learn.
- Inspiring and leading others.
- Watching peoples' faces when they experience an ah-ha moment as a result of something I said to them.
- Being financially stable and comfortable.
- The challenge of a new project that forces me to think.

What I took away from this exercise was that as long as I stuck to these things—and the things I love doing—then the answers to the questions would likely appear.

What I wanted to be when I grew up was a person who could live in the real world and try to influence that world to be as honest as I was attempting to be.

My purpose was to find a way to influence as many people as possible without upsetting my own life balance or keeping me from the things that I loved or that were important to me. And I hoped, through my communication with others, that I just might find a way to impact their lives for the better.

Now it was time to tie that personal vision into the rest of my life.

Part 2 of the Vision

My Life Plan

I took another look at some of the questions I had posed to myself:

- What will be my legacy?
- How does this legacy apply to my family?
- How does it relate to my personal purpose?
- What can I do to help those close to me with their journey to fulfill their purpose?

I reflected on some of the things I had identified as what I loved in life. I thought long and hard about what I wanted to include in my life vision. This part was tough.

I asked myself what significance the people in my life had in relation to my purpose and what I needed to change in terms of these interactions to make myself a better person. When you make a conscious effort to assess aspects of your life like this, then these are the kinds of questions that begin to run through your head.

After some thought, I realized that my vision for my life came down to some simple things:

1. Showing respect for family and friends and supporting them in their journeys. Not thinking I knew what was best for them.
2. Being vulnerable enough to accept love when and if it was presented to me.
3. Having a family of my own and respecting the fact that this has priority over my business aspirations.
4. Realizing that my business is a financial tool in my life; it does not control my life.

5. Living life without expectation and, therefore, without disappointment.
6. Understanding that values equal vision. Living a life of empathy, understanding, compassion, and doing so without judgment.
7. Using my small gifts to help others achieve a better life.

Wonderful notions, aren't they? However, this was the part of my vision that had the greatest potential for ending up in a meaningless frame on a wall. So, in order to help me incorporate these beliefs, I made a personal commitment to reflect on them regularly—if only for a moment—to simply double check on my life values and vision.

I have developed a little routine over the years. On the days I feel I have lived by these values, I try and remember what I did so that I can learn from my actions. On the days I do not, I reflect and think of a young woman who introduced me to many of these things. I remind myself of how she lives her life, how she has taught me to understand these values, and how she reminds me in some way every single day. And I love her for that gift. That always seems to bring back the humility and reminds me to try a little harder the next day.

Now, I know by this stage you might be asking yourself: What has all this got to do with building my business vision and making me a better businessperson?

It has *everything* to do with it.

If you have no personal vision, purpose, legacy, or values, then you can't possibly be responsible enough to own or run a business or to lead others. You need to know where you are going and why you are going there well before you try and work out where your business is going and why. If you're going to run your business—and not have your business run *you*—then you need to make your life all about *you* and not your business. After all, your business is simply the economic force by which you're able to pay for the things you've deemed to be important in life. And I mean *really* important.

Part 3 of the Vision

My Business Plan

I knew that I had to keep everything I had written down in my personal plan and my life plan top-of-mind while creating my business plan:

- My business is my economic driver. It helps me achieve my personal and life vision and to provide for myself and those in my life.
- To succeed, my business must be built on reality.
- I run my business; it does not run me.

As I looked back closely on my career, there was one thing that smacked me in the face like a wet fish on a hot summer's day. I realized that every time I hit the wall and burnt out professionally, my business had been running *me*—instead of the other way around.

I had forgotten that the only real purpose of my career was to pay for the things that I wanted to achieve in life and to fulfill my purpose. To remind myself of this, I put some very specific checks and balances in place to avoid getting sucked back into the business tornado. The simplest of these was to add a very detailed written reminder to myself in my journal about how I felt on the occasions during which I had burnt out. I wrote about the very real and painful emotional, physical, mental, and psychological exhaustion I felt at those times. The experience of reliving those moments—and the emotion it bought forth—is now permanently etched in my memory as a constant reminder to seek balance in life.

Now, instead of simply attempting to feverishly grow my business wherever I can, I look first at what I am seeking personally. I then adjust my business growth and development plan to suit these goals. It's now no longer just about getting more; it's about finding a reason for wanting to get more.

I run my business—and my life—it does not run me.

Interestingly, the outcome of this awareness is that I now find myself with so much more time on my hands to do the things that I want to do in life. I now have time to spend with family and friends, to race, to write, to read, to relax—and simply to love life.

Part 4 of the Vision

My People Plan

- There is no such thing as a self-made millionaire; we build our companies with the help of good people.
- If I am to engage others for help, I need to first understand them.
- How can my business help others achieve *their* vision?
- What milestones can I put in place to keep my business vision and beliefs in check?

You know, I really hate all of the I-did-it-all-myself style business stories. To me that's nothing more than egotistical nonsense. Everyone needs help, or has had help at some stage from *someone*. Years ago, I used to think I was the epicenter of my business success. It wasn't until my business almost *wasn't* a success that I realized I needed the help of those around me. That's when I learned that there is no such thing as self-made.

It was about the same time that I came to appreciate that leading others is way harder than it first seems—particularly when you're under pressure. Everyone loves you when it's "for better"; not so many do when it's "for worse."

I came to understand that I needed to make the fourth part of my vision about those around me. These are the people that I had to engage to help me achieve my vision; to do so, I needed to understand what they wanted from life and what *their* vision was. The easiest way for me to understand that was to have them undergo the same process I did. So each year I asked every one of my staff to describe their own vision in exactly the same way I did: in four parts, with detail for each. I'd sit down and share my vision with them and ask them to do the same with me at our annual staff reviews. This allowed me the opportunity to work some key elements into our business relationship to satisfy everyone's needs.

And finally, the loop was complete. I had vision. And not just vision, but one with purpose. Now I understood how, why, and where *I* was going; and I was in a position to lead others.

Review Your Vision!

Three things you need to do now to Future-Proof Your Business and make sure you really do understand the value of vision.

Action One

Write your own personal vision. Without this, you will never know where you are going or what you want to be when you grow up. Take your time to do this. It's not an easy process and I want you to *consider* each and every answer to the questions you ask yourself.

Action Two

Get your team to write up their personal visions as well. Encourage this by sharing yours with them first. The more open you are with them the more they will be with you, and the greater opportunity you both have to share visions and understand your respective futures.

Action Three

Review your own and your teams' personal visions annually. This is not something you do once. Once done, seek to match those collective personal visions to your business plan and vision and lay this out for all to see so you can all be clear you are aligned.

CHAPTER 5

The Need to Lead

"Leadership has got nothing to do with figuring it out and everything to do with feeling it out. It is an awareness, and for so long I, too, was not aware."

I can recall standing in a conference room of a hotel in Montreal at an Entrepreneurs Organization (EO) university event—one of many I had been to. However, this one was somehow different. We'd just finished a board meeting, one of my first as global president-elect. I was about to really feel what it would be like to take up my global leadership position at the organization. It had been a long day filled with information, discussion, debate, and strategy—and I was beat.

At the time, EO had about 6,500 members. The combined turnover of member businesses was just over $100 billion, the average member age was 36. This group represented the best of young businesspeople and leaders on the planet.

The job for my nine colleagues and me on the Global Board was to lead leaders who lead leaders. The EO leadership infrastructure looked something like this:

- 10 Global Board leaders leading
- 6 regional directors, leading
- 24 area directors, leading
- 108 local chapter residents, leading
- 864 local chapter board members, leading
- 5,500 EO members, leading
- 800,000 EO members' staff

Challenging? You bet. When I asked my predecessor what it was like to be the leader of leaders, he simply replied, "It's like being the only fire hydrant on a street of 6,500 dogs."

And my job was to develop their organization and take it to a better place.

I had just arrived at the evening social function with my counterpart, the EO chairman-elect and co-leader of the organization. Though he and I had met only recently, we'd clicked immediately. We'd parked ourselves next to the bar (a place you could often find us at EO functions) to watch the EO members come into the room for the first social event of the university. In a quiet moment in the corner, we had a little time to ourselves. My chairman turned to me and quietly asked—as 400 members streamed into the room—"What the *heck* have we gotten ourselves into? *We're* supposed to lead these guys!"

We paused for a moment, and I took a deep breath and said, "Okay, here's the thing. We got elected because of who we are and the things we've done for EO over the last decade. These guys consider us to be pretty approachable, open, honest, and real, right?" He looked at me as if to say, okay—where are you going with this?

I took another sip of my wine and continued. "We turn up at functions in jeans instead of suits or blazers, because that's who we are. We talk straight, treat people with respect, and never tell them what to do. We simply help them find a place we think would be better for them and the organization, right?" With trepidation, He responded, "Okay, yeah . . . keep going."

"So, then, let's just keep doing that. Let's not change; let's just be *us*. If we want to turn up in jeans, fine; if we want to be last at the bar, fine; if we want to voice our opinion about their criticisms and comments, that's fine, too. Because that's what they expect from us—people who are real, honest, and open. That's us!"

He paused, smiled, and with a slow nod said, "Yeah, you're right."

He continued after another pause. "And let's not make promises we can't keep. Let's just do a few things well and be able to stand up at the end of the year and know we delivered what we promised. And if we don't have an answer to a question, let's just admit that we don't have the answer and ask that maybe they could help us find one."

I smiled. I was happy. *This* was a real way to lead. At that point, I reckoned we might just pull it off! And I was very aware of what we had to do.

We stood in silence for a moment, finished our drinks, and watched as the members came into the room. We started to smile as I nodded and said, "I think we just worked it out, mate. Our job this year is not to lead. We're just going to keep it as real and honest as possible, and the leadership will come from that."

And that's just what we did. We stood on stage in our jeans a few months later in Washington, D.C., as global leaders of the organization and said, "This is who we are, and this is who you've got as leaders; so come along with us for the ride." We outlined our plans for the organization and explained what we needed them to do with us to make that work. We emphasized how important it was for us to work together and enjoy every moment.

We then set forth a four-point plan that highlighted the things we were going to change in the coming year in an effort to improve the organization. We exited the stage to a standing ovation. I thought to myself as I took my seat in the crowd—*that's* what leadership is all about.

- Open
- Honest
- Real

Fast-forward 12 months to San Francisco and our last address as president and chairman of the North American membership. We spent only a few minutes proudly thanking the leaders and members for their support and passion for their volunteer jobs in the organization. Then we summarized the year that had just passed. There were things we had done and some that were not quite finished, but either way, we left the group in a better place than it had been when we began our terms. And everyone in the room stood to applaud again.

Job well done.

I probably spent about 10 years thinking that just because it was my business, everyone naturally had to play by my rules. I honestly assumed that that's what leading was all about.

Now, of course, I'm sure that most of you are saying, "You dork—of course that's not what it's about! Don't you know anything?"

Well, the fact is, I probably didn't. And the even more pertinent fact is that so many other businesspeople still don't understand leadership, either. They think it's a title or an action or a process, when, in fact, it's a sense of awareness. And for so long, I—like so many others—just wasn't aware.

And, an even *more* humbling fact is that, after a decade of poor leadership, it took a volunteer, not-for-profit leadership role to actually teach me how to become a *true* leader. I had to guide a bunch of volunteers—a group of *entrepreneur* volunteers, at that—*and* get them to do what I wanted them to do, without telling them what to do.

So, let me share one of my most enlightening lessons with you: the lesson of leading.

(And I need to confess that I have only recently been able to articulate and put this lesson into meaningful words in one of my conference presentations.)

There is a seemingly endless number of books about leadership on bookstore shelves all over the world. Many of them offer strategies, rules, plans, and habits that they suggest you adopt to become a good leader. But to me, most of these just seem to spout a load of business rhetoric designed to create *process* leaders as opposed to *people* leaders. I speak from experience, because that's exactly how I was leading for more than a decade. I was a process leader. I read the books, followed the strategies, rules, actions, plans, and processes and figured, ta-da! I've done it. I AM A LEADER . . . SO FOLLOW ME!

I get upset when I come across leadership books written by trainers and other people who have never had experience leading anyone. I also shake my head when I see public speakers tell crowds of people how to lead others, when many of them have spent most of their lives as followers. Their knowledge is not experiential but merely philosophical, as most of these individuals have probably just taken courses (as opposed to earned degrees) in psychology, psychiatry, and adult learning. They've likely come to believe that if they understand the theory behind the process—and talk to enough people about it—then they can understand what it is to be a true leader.

Sorry, but I just don't buy that. For me, leadership has nothing to do with figuring it out, and everything to do with feeling it out. You need to *live* it to learn it.

These are things you can't write down in a strategy nor build a plan around. They're not even items that you can turn into habits. They *are* things you can feel, experience, and develop through your personality and your actions as you learn to become a leader. These are words that mean something to the people you are leading—words that, as a leader, you need to stare at every day and ask: "Do they truly represent who I am? Is that really me?"

My experience as the global president of the Entrepreneurs Organization granted me a variety of leadership lessons—more than I could ever hope to learn in a book. I learned that there is a fine line between confidence and arrogance in a leader. Confidence is driven by ability, truth and honesty; arrogance is based on ego and fear. A confident leader inspires people such that they *want* to be led. An arrogant leader threatens people to follow.

I realized that as long as my fellow leaders and I remained confident, not arrogant, we remained true, that this, in turn, would make it easier to deal with the many issues that we faced, because we only had one reference point: the truth. We didn't waste time looking for ways to dodge the hard questions or sideline the real issues. We tackled them head-on as best we knew how.

The simplicity of this strategy allowed us the time to work on developing core leadership traits to give us a road map for how we should be treating those we lead.

I then honed in on the four key leadership character traits that most true successful leaders possess.:

1. Master
2. Mentor
3. Manager
4. Mate

Let me explain each one in more detail.

Master

The Masters are the *visionaries*, the people who can see around corners and anticipate what's next in both business and life. They do this by understanding the lessons on *how* to *future-proof a business*. In addition, through their considered personal visions, they have learned the lessons and are clear on how to *future-proof themselves*.

Masters trust and live with a keen sense of intuition. They are at one with themselves, in touch with their reality, and aware of who they truly are.

In essence, the Master lives in truth.

Masters have *values* that they've derived from their personal visions and four-part personal plans. Their values keep them in check with themselves and in touch with their reality and stop them from taking shortcuts to get the job done. Leaders never cut corners. They stop at them, look around to see which direction they should take, and then confidently lead their teams around them.

In order to be a leader of the *future*, your vision and values must become part of your personal fabric of *today*.

A Master also shows *vulnerability*. It's a fallacy that a leader needs to hide emotion. That might have been the case 30 to 40 years ago, when everyone thought you needed to be tough to lead. But that's not so anymore. Nowadays, you don't have to be afraid to show your *needs* in order to *lead*.

Members of Generation X—and perhaps even more so, Generation Y—look to their leaders for reality and honesty, and vulnerability comes with that package. It's certainly not a bad thing for a leader to show that he or she is vulnerable, provided that they also put forth solutions. Here's an example from my EO leadership experience and an excerpt from one of the addresses I gave at a U.S. conference:

"We have a great organization, with so many great benefits for members, particularly in North America. My goal this year is to deliver that experience across the planet. To do that we need to formalize how we run the organization everywhere it exists. And I can't do that without your help and experience, as I do not have that local knowledge."

Admitting that I didn't know everything—and asking for the membership to help—clearly showed my vulnerability. I went on.

"I need you to help me understand the unique cultures of your own cities and countries, and help me see how we need to change the organization to suit those cultures—but still retain our core values all over the world. We can do that with your structured feedback and suggestions."

This showed my ability to find and desire to work with others toward a *solution*.

When you exhibit vulnerability, you show others that you are real, human, and that you, too, make mistakes from time to time. This allows members on your team to feel better about the times that they have made mistakes, haven't felt confident, or have been unsure of their direction or vision.

By making your weakness visible to others, you are making it easier for them to show you how you can lead by helping each other.

Mentor

The Mentor is the *teacher*. But of course, to be a teacher, you must first learn what to teach. Teachers must always remain open to learning, and not just from their own mentors and peers but from their subordinates and those they lead as well. Only then will the Mentor be able to join the wealth of knowledge from the old to the potential next big idea of the young.

In other words: Learn how to learn while you teach.

Being a true Mentor also requires that you learn how to share your experiences as opposed to just handing out opinions or advice. Let's face it: Nobody really wants to hear an opinion. Sharing experiences, however, is a means of offering information that others might be able to draw from or to which they may relate. It also allows those who are listening to assess for themselves whether they are right or wrong and grow accordingly. By imparting your experiences, you help your staff learn without feeling as though they are being taught, or that they need to personally experience the same things you did in order to learn. This is one of the key reasons I would ask three questions during my morning calls with employees: How did you do yesterday? What are you focused on today? How can you do it better tomorrow? Their answers allowed me to consider encounters that I had with similar issues. I would then share those experiences with the team so that they could draw from that information and ultimately make their own decisions.

This approach let all team members give me their views on the business without me influencing them with my instructions on how to execute plans. They were able to make up their own minds as to whether I had the *best* way, or just *another* way—or a method that could be improved by mixing it with their own ideas for everyone's benefit.

Mentors are *innovators*; however, they do not need to always innovate on their own. If they have learned how to learn from others, then they've probably seen that some of the best innovations come from collaborative ideas. New ideas sometimes come from new people.

The Mentor is a *motivator*; I have a very strong belief when it comes to motivation, and that is that you cannot directly motivate others. You can only motivate them to motivate themselves. I'm often referred to as a "motivational speaker" and I hate it. I am never going to motivate someone directly. I might be able to motivate people to figure out ways to inspire *themselves* by sharing my experiences and actions. After all, most audiences typically listen to me speak for only an hour or so, then they get back to their lives. I'm not going to be there when their alarms go off at 5 A.M. the next day, or when they are in a slump, sitting in their offices with the doors shut, or when they are having a tough time with their families because they are not spending enough time with them.

That's not my job. In fact, it's not anyone else's job. The responsibility belongs to each and every one of us in relation to our self-motivation. My job is to at least have people take a look at themselves and the true potential they have in life, such that they might act on those thoughts.

Only you can motivate you.

True Mentors will be able to explain the personal habits and experiential actions they take to motivate themselves in the belief that their subordinates will learn from this and develop their own self-motivating methods.

Manager

The Manager personality is all about *action*—and not that of your staff or those you are to lead. It's about your *own* actions, because this will determine how *they* act. True Managers need to have discipline, because *your* discipline encourages discipline in others, just as your respect encourages respect in others.

I spent a long time as a Manager operating under the belief that issuing instructions to subordinates meant that I was doing enough to manage them. It was not until I realized that I needed to follow my *own* instructions first that I gained the respect of those I was leading and was able to truly be in a management position.

I look back on some of the stupid things I did when I first started to manage staff. I'd gather them all for a morning briefing on a project, tell them that the deadline was tight and we all had to chip in and pull our weight, then slip out the door myself at noon and head to a boozy lunch for the rest of the afternoon with a bunch of mates. There is no discipline or respect in *any* of those actions, and they certainly do not escape notice

Now don't get me wrong; I still love to head out every now and again with my mates for a big afternoon on the drink, talking rubbish to each other and playing up like secondhand lawnmowers. However, I've now learned how to share the love while managing others. Now, if the work is on, so am I. If the work is not, and none of us are under the gun, then we *all* take a break—not just me.

In order to be clear with yourself on whether you are truly managing through your own actions, I want you to stop for a moment, reflect on your last three months as a leader, and ask yourself these questions:

- How often do you set a meeting and then fail to show up for it yourself?
- Do you make rules in your business that you don't follow, yet you expect others to?
- Do you ask others to have a routine or process but don't have one yourself?
- Do you manage by example (truth and reality) or instruction (ego and fear)?

Unless *you* have discipline first—unless *you* have earned respect first—you cannot possibly expect either from the members of your team.

The first time I took a long, hard look at the way I was managing, I realized that *I* was, in fact, my worst team member. I'd miss meetings, I didn't have a schedule or routine, I wouldn't follow my own rules, and I spent too much time offering instruction and not displaying action.

Once I developed a stronger sense of discipline, however, I was in a position to consider how I would engage and empower others to complete the task. As is often the case with routine and discipline, I experienced the benefit of more free time in my day. And having the time to manage is particularly important if you are to stay one step in front of your subordinates.

Mate

Everyone likes to be liked, and those in the position of leader are no different. You don't want to be the bad guy, the bloke nobody wants to work for or with. You want to be seen as the leader who people want to follow.

The Mate persona is a particularly tough one to balance. You need to be friendly but firm, empathetic to everyone's life drama, yet distant enough not to become *part* of that drama. If you get too "matey," you risk losing your team's respect by becoming too familiar as an equal. Not "matey" enough, and they're likely to see you as aloof, controlling, and not in touch with your teams' needs.

One of the great tools I have used to assist my own development of the "mate trait" is encouraging my team members to prepare their personal vision. I use this tool as a means to find out more about their lives, what makes them tick, what is important to them, and how I can work with that in the business.

It's easy to assume that we know what our staff members want from their careers or lives. It's another thing to actually *ask* them and really listen to the answers. I used to think money was the key to all things in business. Of course that's what your employees want—more money, right?

Nope. Not always.

My employees were an interesting mix. For some, the hot button was money, for others, it was travel. Some simply wanted a faster computer or more office supplies to make their jobs easier. There were the party animals who just wanted to work hard and play hard and drink the boss's booze. And there were those whose desires were deeper and who were truly focused on personal development and improvement.

We found a way to make it work for each of them and be empathetic and understanding to their needs. We didn't just focus on what they wanted today, but tomorrow and in the days and weeks to come, as well. This allowed me to plan for both my future *and* their future.

When I asked my long-time personal assistant about her personal plan for the coming year, she informed me that she wanted to go back to school and study to become a nurse. So the two of us worked out a plan that worked for both of us and moved each of us toward achieving our life goals. When another employee revealed that she wanted to travel for 12 months, we figured out a way to remove her from the business over the next 6 months. The result was a better transition to her moving on and someone else moving in, which again made life easier for both of us.

It's not hard to work out the mate trait; it just takes a little understanding and empathy. A key to this role is to remember that if you don't show you care, they won't either.

Being a leader is tough. I've come to strongly believe—after more than two decades of being a leader of staff and a decade of being a leader of leaders—that

---

Leaders are not born; they evolve. And to evolve, you must first be aware.

To help keep myself in check, I've put together a little list of questions that I often ask myself. These are the things I use to pull myself back when I feel like I have wandered off track or lost touch with those I am leading. It's my way of looking from the outside in at how others perceive my abilities as a leader. To give you a bit of a head start on creating your own

list, I've put a copy of those questions in the workbook section
for you.

Review Your Leadership!

*Three things you need to do now to Future-Proof Your
Business to make sure you truly understand the need to
lead.*

Action One

Before you can truly understand the *need to lead* you must first
understand all of the lessons to *future-proof* both yourself and
your business. This is the platform from which great leaders
are built.

Action Two

Leaders are aware. Are you aware of what surrounds you on
a daily basis? Remember, leadership is about feeling it out,
not figuring it out; you have to live it to learn it.

Action Three

Stop and assess yourself on the four key leadership character
traits: the Master, Mentor, Manager, and Mate. Look for
ways to develop them in your daily leadership life.

Don't get too cocky when you feel you have mastered the
four key character traits. Remember that there is a fine line
between confidence and arrogance, so make a daily effort to
keep your ego in check.

6

I'm Done!

"I was four businesses into my private enterprise career before I figured I'd better start working out how long I should be in that business, if I was ever going to find a way out of it in the future."

How long do you expect to be in business? Do you know? Have you even thought about it? Or, did you just wake up one day and boom—you were in business—and now you're just too focused on surviving each day to even consider what the future may bring?

When I first started in business, all I really ever cared about was what was happening today, or more accurately, how we were going to get through today without going broke. Tomorrow was all about bigger, better, harder, faster . . . *more!* As for the future, well, I just figured it would take care of itself, so long as I kept the pedal to the metal.

Why? I don't know; it just sounded like that plan would work, I guess.

However, despite the fact that I wanted bigger/better/ harder/faster tomorrow, I was not really considering what the effects that my actions today had on my tomorrow. And more significantly I wasn't aware of how some of the decisions I was making might come back to haunt me in the future.

I look back to my first real business and remember going into it with starry-eyed, reckless abandon and romantic notions. I was going to live happily ever after, and my newfound business love would surely last a lifetime. My mother (and business partner at the time) did her best to keep my feet on the ground and offer a solid dose of reality in the business, but despite her constant reminders, my enthusiasm sometimes got in the way of common sense. My second business adventure was my recording studio that I built with a mate, and given audio production was my passion, this business was my field of dreams.

I had the same blind enthusiasm and ridiculous thought that "If I build it, they will come."
  But of course, they didn't!

Mere months into the recording business we were bleeding like we'd had a full body shave with a blunt razor—and the bank certainly did not put its hand out to offer a transfusion. In fact, it didn't even give us a Band-Aid. That's one of the biggest problems that people encounter when starting a new business. While *you* trust in yourself and your ability, others could not care less and will happily step over your cold, dying body in the street in favor of running after their own dreams of the future.

It wasn't until a few years later that I figured out where I went wrong—and the truth is that it was well before I even started. I was getting into businesses without a clue about when and how I would get out of them, least of all how I would create or even be able to identify that exit point. I just figured that one day the business would either stop, or that someone would magically come along and buy it from me for a stupid amount of money.

I think the bad habits set in when I began the property business. I had inadvertently established a system where the "exit" was always the sale of the house; it was an individual *asset* exit rather than a company exit. So, when we actually built a real business with overheads and offices and people and all the good gear to go with it, it was an entirely different story that required a different attitude. All of a sudden, we had a more permanent commitment and an actual company to run, rather than just doing daily business out of the front seat of a pickup, with our "business tools" thrown in the back.

I was four businesses into my private enterprise career before I realized that I'd better start determining how long I should be in that business if I was ever going to find a way out of it. To think I had come that far and didn't have an exit strategy for any of them frightened me. I felt a bit like the guy who never got out of the mail room, mainly because he could not see a way out.

I've since come to learn that hardly anybody really thinks about an exit strategy upon entry. Yet without a plan for one, you can't help but get caught in the self-fulfilling *Groundhog Day* prophecy, as one day slides into the next with the only real purpose being survival.

Working as a business consultant for so many years, I've come to understand how many professionals suffer from what can only be described as a bad marriage with their business. They get into business originally because of the romantic notion of working for themselves. They have stars in their eyes leading up to the big day and can only focus on the moment when they will tie the knot and open the doors to their new adventure. It's a moment full of wonder, excitement, pride, and the childlike fantasy of a new beginning.

The big day comes and goes, and they head into the honeymoon period and the euphoria that comes with not having to answer to a boss. And then, all of a sudden, the responsibility of this new relationship sets in. They soon realize that though they may not have a boss, they *do* have banks, landlords, creditors, staff, clients, and nervous spouses to answer to. In business as in marriage, it requires work and ongoing effort to maintain and develop. The itches soon set in and they begin to wonder what the hell they got themselves into.

It's just not fun anymore.

It's about this time that the daily grind of *Groundhog Day* begins. These diligent professionals go through the same motions each day, drowning under the weight of the issues they need to deal with, completely clueless as to how to keep the marriage to their business intact. And, as a result, sometimes the dream business marriage ends in a messy and ugly divorce, as they simply give up on the dream and decide to take a different path in life. And oftentimes this hard decision is made too late; the financial and emotional damage has already been done, futures are lost, and lives have been shattered.

There *is* a way around this, though. You just need to keep it real, and start with the end in mind.

After a few failed attempts, I finally figured out that there was simply *no way* to lead my business toward any sort of purpose without knowing what it was supposed to look like when it was finished. I needed to determine how to get *out* of my businesses before I got *into* them.

On the back of a solid and structured business plan I needed to hypothesize an exit, or even alternative exits, and then look as far into the future as I could to work back to each and every influence that life could deal me to potentially change that future, good and bad. That assessment and clarity of vision could mean that I simply didn't get into the business in the first place; otherwise, I may risk being stuck in a bad business marriage forever!

This is a very real problem for business owners all over the world. Without an exit strategy and vision, they can easily become slaves to their businesses. I was very lucky to learn this lesson reasonably early in my business career; it helped me set up a formula for all of our future investments.

I have done my best to follow the simple rule to never fall in love with an asset.

Assets do not define me, control me, or run my life. They are simply there to help me make a buck to pay for the things in life that *are* important to me—those I've identified as such in my personal plan. That—and that alone—is their purpose. That's what all of my business interests do for me. That's why there will come a time when I can leave them and let them go.

So how do you know when it's time to move on to the next business adventure in life? I personally use an exit *formula*. This is more than just a financial formula; it's a mix of finance, emotion, and intuition. Each of our business interests has an exit formula that represents a process for us to follow so that we know when the business has grown up for us and it's time to move on. And when I say "we," I mean *all* of our staff in the business.

Of course, I'm looking for the best possible way to leave the business, so I need the best possible people working on that departure plan. These aren't individuals who work outside the business, but rather people who are already in it, running it. This means I need to display openness, honesty, and incentive.

Each staff member in every one of our business interests knows our exit formula for that business and when we expect to put the plan into effect. There is no need to lie to any of them. Making them aware of my vision allows them to match their personal plans to that vision. And somewhere in the middle, we can both serve a purpose for each other.

Being open and honest encourages dialogue that allows us to better identify opportunities. For example, I might need to share an opportunity with staff members for short-term financial reward as we build the business quickly for a trade sale or identify an opportunity for a management buyout of the business. Or, I may want to explain how they could position themselves as key players to be hired by the new management when the business is sold. By understanding where opportunities arise and sharing them with one another, we can help each other achieve our goals and, in turn, fulfill our personal plans and visions.

Our formula is certainly not rocket science. In fact, over the years, it's become more of a checklist. It's not just a checklist for me, either; it's for my teams, and in some instances, the shareholders with whom we have partnered on a business project. These are the serious, hand-on-our-heart questions that we ask ourselves, and answering them helps to reveal the formula and exit date.

Question 1. *What is the life cycle of this business category, and where is the business positioned in that cycle?*
Every business category has a life cycle of peaks and troughs. This cycle is driven by a number of influencers, such as:

- Economic environment
- Political environment
- Product or service development
- Technology development
- Research discoveries
- Available professionals to work in that category
- Historic trends
- Category growth idiosyncrasies
- Product or service positioning in the market

In order to know when to get out of a business, one must know at what point of the business cycle you are getting in.

I spend a lot of time mapping cycles to fully understand how long it will be before a particular category or business peaks.

Our formula for pinpointing a sale time is to set up the business to be trading at its optimum just before the cycle peaks. Always seek to sell on the upward trend, not at the peak. Typically, if you are at the peak, you're already beginning to decline; you just can't see it yet.

You can often see this problem in the field of hospitality, specifically in restaurants. As restaurants build up over time, the normal cycle of growth takes its course. The restaurant often becomes a popular spot after a given period, but with popularity comes hard work for someone who is typically both an owner and a manager. This individual hangs on for "one more season" just to make the most out of his hard work, only to become tired and jaded with the industry, and grumpy on a daily basis. The now unpleasant boss prompts the waitstaff and servers to slack off; the best chef snaps and walks out the back door throwing pots and pans at unsuspecting homeless people in the back alley; and the *sous-chef* just can't cut it because he puts more brandy in his coffee than he does into the dishes he's creating. While it might not be apparent to the now industry-numb owner, the restaurant has been deteriorating for weeks. In a moment of tired frustration and a declaration that this is just "all too hard," the owners spit the dummy and announce that they are going to sell. But the cancer has already begun to spread, and the word on the street is that this place is not what it used to be. Patrons are already beginning to shift camp, and the once opportune moment to capitalize on the sale of a great business on exit is lost.

If you always look to sell on the upward trend you leave a little bit on the table for the next owners, so that they can see growth opportunities and development potential in the business. You want the buyer to feel like they can make it bigger/better/faster than what you were able to achieve. It's like a dog marking its territory. "Yeah, you guys did a great job to get the business here, but stand back, because we're going to show you how it's really done. We're going to make this place rock."

And I *love* that they want to do that. That is exactly the buyer profile I want, because

---

Ego will always pay more for a business than ability.

Question 2. *What are the triggers for the "fun factor" in the business?*

Burnout comes about in business in a number of forms—believe me, I've seen most of them, and lived a few myself. The easiest one to identify occurs when a business owner or operator is just not enjoying getting out of bed every day, and you hear these words come out of their mouth: "It's just not fun anymore."

To counter this in each of our business interests, I attempted to identify what could take the fun out of the business—and then set some parameters in order to stay aware of these things. This way, if we ever felt like we were losing the fight, we could reconsider and possibly expedite our exit plans. Here are some of our real-life examples.

Our consulting business predominantly worked with clients in the franchise sector. Since we started this business almost two decades ago, we saw that it was part of a growth sector and that we had an opportunity to get in on the upward cycle. But, we got in well before franchising was popular, so for the first 10 years, we essentially ate baked beans and slept in cardboard boxes. It was *tough*. The trigger we put in place here was a particular date. I determined approximately how long I could afford to starve and matched this to the sector's growth cycle of the previous five years. If I was not living a certain lifestyle by the date I set, then we'd get out. And wouldn't you know it—*just* as the date was arriving, franchising took off. Had this not been the case, we would have gotten out of the business before I burned out, since it just wouldn't have been fun anymore.

The trigger in our property development business was interest rates. We had a great run in the property market for a good period of time. But, like most businesspeople, we still needed to watch our costs, and one of the biggest ones we had was holding costs. I picked an interest rate percentage that I felt was sustainable in the business. Anything beyond that percentage would have made trading tough and certainly stressful and, therefore, definitely not fun anymore. And as soon as the rate hit that number, we started getting out of all of our investments. Interestingly, the cycle was still well on an upward trend at the time, with some way to run. But the economic and political environment had changed, and the impact of these events was looming just over the horizon. We got out with only one minor casualty—a small loss on one of our properties. Other similar businesses around us took a much bigger hit, and, in some instances, hit the wall because their only trigger was greed.

It really does not matter *what* your fun factor is in business, just that you've taken the time to *identify* what it is in your business.

Each and every one of our businesses revolves around relationships with clients, suppliers, creditors, and staff. Any displeasure you have with yourself or your situation is reflected in those relationships; and this, in turn, creates stress in the workplace. And stress can't help but have a negative impact on your business development and plans for your company's future. And that's why business has got to be fun!

For me, it's easy: If the fun has gone, then it's time for the business to go, too.

Question 3. *How quickly can we add value to the business?* This is an important part of the formula for me. It's one thing to grow the business organically and add value. However, I need to identify clever methods to add value *quickly* if I am to make the most of the business through its business cycle on the path to exit. So I ask myself the following questions.

- What intellectual property can I develop for the business that will help leverage our product or service offer in the future, or that will deliver a futuristic product or service today?
- How can we add an annuity element to the company's sales development?
- What recurring revenue, or referral revenue elements, can we cultivate to help the business sell itself to our clients or customers?
- What is currently stopping this business from being the success it could be? What people or resources do I need to add to the business to overcome that impasse?
- What are my realistic timelines for achieving all of these things?

The answers to these questions help make it clear to me just how quickly I can realistically add value to the business. I can then overlay that time frame to the business cycle and the business's position in the cycle. This allows me to forecast the speed of achievable business development relative to the window of opportunity I have for achieving that development which, in turn, offers me a more feasible exit date and value.

Pretty straightforward, really, when you think about it!

The last part of the formula is money. What do we expect to return on this business, both annually, and on exit?

Question 4. *How much is enough?*
My financial formula for building and exiting a business is not about how much I can get; its more about how much is enough.

You might remember Michael Douglas's character Gordon Gekko, and his famous line from the movie *Wall Street*: "The point is, ladies and gentlemen, is that greed—for lack of a better word—is good. Greed is right. Greed works. Greed clarifies, cuts through, and captures the essence of the evolutionary spirit."

And that kind of attitude is *exactly* what landed Mr. Gekko in jail!

For me, it's all about enough. And enough is to never be so egotistical as to ask *too much*.

But how do you know it's enough? Some accountants will say the formula needs to be a return on asset, or a return on funds invested, or just a profitability multiplication formula. And they would all be right in different circumstances for different reasons with different businesses. Me, I have my own formula, and it's one that I reckon is pretty simplistic and realistic. I am for sure no accountant or financial advisor, nor do I ever put myself out to be one. I am just a simple bloke who understands simple things, and this is just my way of getting my head around how I monetize my exit.

I break my financial exit formula down into two parts.

1. What dollar figure would be enough for me as an annual return on investment, in relation to:
   a. The state of the business when I bought it?
   b. The market environment for the business if it is a start-up?
   c. Our investment, if I was simply as a non-controlling shareholder?
2. What figure would be enough for me to exit the business in relation to:
   a. The length of time I intend to hold on to the business asset?
   b. The relative risk of staying in the business beyond the cycle, or longer than our forecast exit date?
   c. The availability of buyers?

In relation to an *annual* return, we'd ask ourselves the qualifying questions and typically seek to achieve a 20 to 25 percent annual EBIT (Earnings Before Interest and Taxes) as a return on investment. I sought out business and market environments that accommodated that outcome. If I were to achieve anything less than that annually, then the business would want to look like it's going to return a stellar result on exit to compensate for the shortfall on the annual dividends, or I might as well deposit the cash into the bank or my retirement fund and not worry about any risk.

On *exit* we would ask ourselves the qualifying questions and then overlay the following fairly straightforward formula just to help us assess if we felt we had achieved our financial hurdle of "enough":

4　× EBIT minimum
　+ goodwill (calculated as 10% of EBIT)
　+ real tangible assets (items such as real property/
　　　real estate/any substantial intellectual property)
　= sale price

Using this simple formula—and knowing that we had bought the business well and paid *just enough* for it in the first place, had worked hard *enough*, planned *enough*, were honest *enough*, and employed people who were real *enough*—made us feel sure that we'd be able to engineer *enough* for the business on exit.

It was rare for me to hold a business for longer than seven years, for two reasons. One is that many businesses see a category or financial cycle within seven years, and another is that owners tend to get the famous seven-year itch and become bored and uninterested with the business. This would help us understand length of time in the business versus the risk of staying on in the business.

And last but certainly not least, my lesson on exit was to always take the intuitive offer as opposed to the egotistical offer.

It's always okay to leave something on the table for the next guy in favor of not getting anything to the table and ultimately starving yourself.

Review Your Exit!

Three things you need to do now to Future-Proof Your Business and make sure you really do know when you are done.

Action One

Figure out what your business will look like when it is done or when you are done with it. Write this down and review your position regularly with your own formulas that suit your life situation.

Action Two

Work out how much is enough for you to make—and set your clear sights to make an exit. Never fall in love with an asset.

Action Three

Check your exit plan against your personal plan, and determine whether the two of them align. Your vision and values need to match your exit plan.

PART

III

Reality Check

CHAPTER

7

The Information Age

"In order to take information onboard we need to let go of our ego. Absorbing information is all about humility."

When I first started in business, I thought that being competitive simply meant being better than the next guy in your chosen field. But the truth is that it's not so much about being better as it is about being *smarter*. And the only way to get smarter is with information.

I'd watch people who started their businesses around the same time that I did fly past me as they built their companies—and I'd wonder how they were doing it. What was I missing? I was good at what I did; I worked the hours, put in the hard yards. I figured that if I worked twice as hard, I'd cover twice as much ground in the same space of time. But all I seemed to be doing was spinning my wheels twice as fast at the start line.

The answer to my question was simple: These people had better *information* than I and their other competitors did. That helped them not only *predict* the future and develop enhanced strategies to match that vision to grow their businesses at an accelerated pace, it helped them bring the future to *them!*

It took me years of beating my head against a brick wall and fighting the good fight to learn that if I wanted to get ahead of my competitors, my real challenge was to look for information to which my competitors did not have access. If I was only getting the same amount and quality of information as my competitors, then I could only expect to come up with the same strategies that they did. It sounds simple when you think about it; I just didn't think about it!

Then I thought to myself—maybe I just wasn't asking *the right* questions. It suddenly struck me that I wasn't asking *any* questions.

One of the biggest barriers in our search for answers usually stems from our fear of asking questions—fear that is typically driven by ego.

Ego is like a huge hand brake when it comes to gathering information and learning. It clouds your judgment about what is wrong or right, true or false, as you tend to believe solely in your own view. We've all heard the line that people are "starting to believe in their own BS." That's simply ego kicking in; it occurs when businesspeople stop listening and start selling themselves. It's like a filter that says, "Yeah, I'm listening to you, but I still think I'm right." They listen, but they don't hear.

In order to properly receive new material, we need to let go of our egos. Absorbing information is all about humility.

But developing a sense of humility in business is a little harder than one might think. You see, we all want to look *smart*, and appear to know what we are doing. We want to look like we are a success. But the truth is that without humility, you can never be a success. It took me a *long* time to learn that; and it wasn't until I let go of my ego and achieved a sense of humility, compassion, and understanding that I actually started to make a buck. I finally began to understand how to view the value of the information I was handed—and how to absorb it adequately—when I learned how to be the following three things:

1. **Humble:** I had to come to terms with the fact that I can't do it all on my own. As I stated before, there is no such thing as a self-made millionaire; we all need, or have, help from someone at some time. Ask others for help and information, and feel good about the fact that you asked. If you accept success humbly by acknowledging others' help, success will come more easily. You'll be surprised just how many people *want* to help if you just ask them.

2. **Compassionate:** I realized that if I'm going to ask others for help, then I need to be compassionate and serve *their* needs as well. It is not about what they can do for me, but rather what we can do for each other.

3. **Understanding:** Understanding how others view the world will put you in a better position to understand how you should view the information they have to offer. Be accepting of their views and their values as opposed to being judgmental. Judgment is driven by ego.

When I was finally able to grasp these notions and actually started to apply them to my life, things changed dramatically for me, both personally and professionally. In fact, I reckon that my ego probably cost me over one million dollars in my early business years—all because I was too proud to ask questions. And it certainly wasn't one of my proudest moments to admit that! I am honestly amazed at my own foolishness. Now, some 20 years later, I'll ask strangers in the street for help if I do not have the answers.

Next to people, information is your greatest asset in business.
It is the fuel for development.

Without information, you simply cannot grow. But
there are some things for you to consider when gathering
information:

- **What** information do you specifically need?
- **Where** are you going to get that information from?
- **What** are you going to do with the information once you
  have it?

There have been some very specific people and places I can
pinpoint as sources of information. After I learned to put my
ego in my pocket, I sat down and made a list of the things I
wanted to learn about. I then set about determining exactly
where I could get that information in the future. Here's a quick
rundown of the things we realized we had to address in order
for us to *future-proof* our information.

All Information Comes at a Price

Frustration led me to this lesson. I got sick of being the guy
at the barbeque listening to stories of how someone closed a
great deal or found a new product, came up with an innovative
business strategy that outsmarted his competitors, shook up
the market, or did something amazing for his business. I kept
leaving these conversations asking myself, "How *did* he do that?
And why can't I seem to work that out?"

So I started to set a budget each year for my "information
and learning fund," and I even went so far as to have our financial team put the money into a separate account. This ensured
that no matter how tough the cash flow situation looked, I

would still have money to go out into the world and learn more to make us a better organization. And I do mean go out into the world. I figured that if I was to gain access to information that my competitors did not have, well, then I needed to travel to places they probably would not go in order to find it.

Your learning fund does not need to have a lot of money in it; it just needs to be used wisely. Mine started out as only $200 a week, or about $10,000 a year. My first fund got me to one overseas conference a year as well as a few annual magazine subscriptions—typically for publications that I could not get at a newsstand. And that's where we started. Now, our budget for my information and learning fund is way more than that. I look to get to at least two conferences a year, have membership in a number of organizations where I can network and learn, and subscribe to various publications from around the world.

Too often I hear small businesspeople say they can't *afford* to learn. "Yeah, I'd like to go to that seminar, but I just can't afford it." But the simple fact is that you can't afford *not* to learn.

Network

We've all heard it said that to be successful in business, you need to network. We've been told time and again that "your net-work is your net-worth." But in reality, your network is only as good as the worth you can create for others with whom you network. It's certainly *not* all about you!

Networking doesn't just mean that you attend functions, shake hands, and kiss babies, or answer the simple question about what you do for a living. Networking requires that you harness the true value of the people you meet. I'm sure that many of you have read countless books on how to be a better networker or how to take advantage of the connections around you. But I don't think it has to be complicated. I just learned to put a few rules in place to help derive value from networking.

Rule 1: Network in the Nude

Don't try to be what you are not. Be who you *are*, not who you think you need to be.

Take off the emperor's clothing to be the true you. People relate to real; just be yourself.

I can remember my boss coming into the studio after my first on-air shift as a young radio announcer. He sat quietly in front of me and asked, "How do you reckon it went last night?" Still excited from my first on-air experience, I responded, "I think I did okay." He paused, and in a very quiet voice said, "You did well last night, but I need you to bring Troy to work with you. Troy got you the job, and Troy is the one I want to hear on-air. You are not a different person at work. You are the same person that you are at home; that's what will keep you real to others. And that's why I hired you."

I learned my lesson right then and there; I wasn't doing anyone any favors by pretending to be someone I wasn't. From that moment on, I realized how important it was to keep it real.

Rule 2: Not All Networks Work

Choose your networks carefully and be discriminating. Not all of the opportunities presented to attend functions or join groups will be helpful to you. Look for those that you feel will give you the most value or to which you can offer the most value. This will keep you from becoming discouraged with networking as you purposefully create a more positive outcome from the specific groups you pursue.

Rule 3: Be Pitch Perfect

Prepare your elevator pitch, the 30-second answer to "What do you do for a living?" or "What's your business?" And here is the networking key: Construct your answer so that it will encourage a conversation that is a little more personal and not just superficial. After all, the person you have just met might be shy about starting conversations and not know what to say next. If you merely go through the motions of networking by using the standard, "What do you do? How do you do that? Where do you do that? Wow, that must be interesting blah blah blah"—then the conversation stops pretty quickly.

I can remember a time just after we'd built our recording studio. Our core business focus was to create advertising jingles for advertising agencies. Through one of my mother's friend's contacts, I jagged an invite to a Christmas party at the home of one of the biggest advertising agency bosses in the country. This was a *huge* opportunity for me. I was going to get the chance to network with 150 of the country's top advertising executives. They were *the* most influential people that I could find, all in one spot at one time, many of them with information that could catapult my business to the next level.

And I *blew it*!

I arrived at the function dressed for the part, and ready to *be* what I *thought* they wanted me to be. I really thought I had it together. But I was completely unprepared. While I thought that I knew what I was going to say, I hadn't really given much thought to what I might be asked—or what I needed to ask them to keep others interested in the conversation and in me. In short, I had not studied my subjects nor really understood the audience that I was about to engage.

Consequently, from the moment I walked into the party, I knew I was way out of my league. And to make matters worse, once I realized that, that's exactly how I came across—like a scared kid. These guys knew how to work a room and seek out those who they needed to engage and extract information from.

They were also able to politely move on from the conversations that were not delivering on those needs.

I had not really worked out what I could do for these people; I had only been concentrating on what I felt they could do for *me*. There was no reciprocation in the conversation, which ultimately left me sounding like I was there hunting for business—something that very quickly resulted in me standing in the corner about as comfortable as a priest at a swingers' party.

Rule 4: Engagement Comes through the Art of Conversation, not Solicitation

Now, many years later, I've learned that there are three parts to engaging those with whom you wish to network:

1. Make it about them.
2. Make it meaningful.
3. Make it memorable.

And these three things start right from the moment you're asked that ever-popular opening question: "So, what do you do for a living?"

Here's an example of how to get it wrong. "So, what do you do, Troy?" "I'm a public speaker and author. I speak about business, marketing, and leadership topics." This can only lead to the expected, "Oh wow, that must be exciting" comment or the inevitable, "Oh, so you're a motivational speaker then." And I *really* hate the label "motivational speaker."

Beginning conversations in this way usually leads to a string of superficial sentences from both parties, where people talk *at* each other and not *with* each other. The next time you're at a networking function, take a look around the room at the individuals engaged in conversations. It's almost as though you can see their lips moving, but nobody is really interested in what is coming out of their mouths. I call it "commercial deafness." It's the moment when you become aware that you truly don't care about the answer to your question, even before the person you are conversing with has given it, and then your inner voice starts to talk to you. "I know I should be listening, but I am really just not that interested." And then your mind wanders back to that new racecar, as you search for an exit and another glass of wine.

These conversations become very question-and-answer-oriented, quite routine, and fairly boring. Nobody is sharing or learning anything of importance or appeal. They typically end very quickly when one party feels like there is nothing to be gained from the individual to whom he is speaking. Someone inevitably hands over a business card in the faint hope that some business might materialize from the exchange someplace down the road.

However, if you follow these basic rules of engagement, you can't help but instigate more of a real conversation. You'll find that you are both inspired to look a little more closely at each other and perhaps see if there might be more to learn or more information to gather. A more meaningful conversation will also reveal a possible second or third degree of separation that might assist you with yet another important contact.

Here's how it works when you play by the four simple networking rules of engagement.

"So, what do you do, Troy?" "I'm a public speaker and author; I speak about business, leadership, and marketing topics. Have you heard any good speakers lately?" (Remember: It's about *them*.) This then leaves me open to ask questions like: Why did you like that particular speaker? What were some of the key ideas that you got from the presentation? How did you apply those in your business? What led you to the speaker in the first place? Another approach is to share something like, "This is who I saw last week, and these are some of the ideas that I got from the presentation." The personal interest aspect of the questions tells the person you are speaking to that you really are interested in him—and not just what he can do for you. And this is how you make it *meaningful*.

And finally, to make it *memorable*, share something that you know will stick with the person. "So, the big gem I got from the whole presentation was. . . ."

Break it down; make it personal; make it real; follow the rules of engagement; and you'll find an easier path to break through to the information and truly make your network add value to your net worth.

Join Groups or Organizations

One of the greatest things I have done in business was to join the Entrepreneurs' Organization (EO), a group that gave me perspective and a wealth of information to help me in my business. EO (www.eonetwork.org) is composed of thousands of businesspeople from across the planet who all own their own businesses. All of the companies turn over more than $1 million in revenue, and all members are under the age of 50.

When I was first invited to join the organization in 1996, my ego was still running my business. I thought to myself, "Nope, not interested; I don't need this. Thanks, but no thanks." But since my friend Tom had been the one to suggest I join EO, I felt some obligation to at least *listen* to the gentleman to whom he was trying to introduce me to talk about the organization. A few phone calls later, I was invited to an information session in a private cellar of an exclusive club in the city. *Now* they had my attention!

I went into the meeting thinking that even if I didn't join EO, at least I got to hang out with some cool guys, listen to their stories for a few hours, and drink some sensational wine (the kind I usually could not afford). And that didn't sound so terrible, right?

So I went along, and after we'd consumed the first bottle of wine, they had my complete interest in the organization. After the second bottle, they had my credit card to join; and after the third bottle I found myself elected to the local board as founding chapter president.

And I never looked back!

A while later I was invited to join the Asia Pacific board of EO. My first board meeting in Tokyo was an event that would change my life and my direction in business forever.

I can recall sitting in the boardroom in a wonderful hotel in Tokyo Beach looking back over the city of Tokyo and thinking to myself, "How did I get *here?*" As the morning went on and I listened to some of the stories in the room, I did some mental calculations. Nine other EO members were in the room, with an average age of about 33 and an estimated combined worth of about a half a billion dollars. And then there was me, at the end of the table, with my eclectic and oh-so-average group of businesses that stumbled to where they are today—and a hole in my sock, to boot.

Yup! That's all I could think of. "You have a hole in your sock, you moron—you are *way* out of your league here! I think it's time for you to pull your head in, shut up, and listen. It's time to put your ego in your pocket, get real, get humble, and learn from these men and women, because these people are sharp!"

As the day wore on my ego took a total hammering—one that it rightfully deserved. Each smart idea that came out of my fellow board members' mouths reminded me of another dumb thing I'd done over the last decade. It was like someone in the business universe had a little Troy voodoo doll that he was jamming with pins every other minute to remind me of the business sins that I had committed as a result of total and unabashed big-headed stupidity.

The torture's culmination came at dinner. There we were, at the fine dining restaurant within the hotel, ready to enter our private dining room overlooking the Tokyo lights, with full, exclusive chef and table service, and of course, in traditional Japanese fashion, we had to take off our shoes.

In an effort to prevent my total embarrassment and the revelation of the hole in my sock, I faked the need to go to my room and get a camera so I could capture the evening's events. I hurriedly slipped upstairs to my room to find some less offensive and intact foot covering. I came back to the table suitably clothed but without an excuse for not having a camera in hand (notwithstanding that I didn't even own one).

The final blow had been dealt. My inner self officially declared me thick as a brick. And although I was a beaten man, I was one now ready to absorb information and prepare for the much brighter future ahead as a result. I was in my truth.

Later that night I retreated to my room to sit in the dark and stare at the lights of Tokyo and consider what was next in my life. It was amazing. It was almost as though I'd been playing from the bench for the last 10 years, *thinking* I was on the team, but now I had the chance to actually run on and *play*.

I spent many of the years that followed on EO regional and global boards. My time in EO culminated with a term as the 2006–2007 EO global president, an experience I will tell you about soon.

It was a truly incredible and humbling ride.

So what was my lesson? Find and become a member of an organization that suits you—but don't just show up. Get involved, jump into it with both feet, and fully experience it. I used to say to EO members all over the world, "There is no value in EO. There are many benefits the organization has to offer; what you choose to do with them will ultimately give you the value."

Attend Learning Events

Each year, I seek out at least two conferences to attend somewhere in the world. I don't go there to speak but to simply participate and learn. After all, how can I possibly teach others if I am not constantly learning myself? I use my Christmas break every year to take a moment to consider what I might need to learn in the coming 12 months and then set about finding an appropriate event to attend. It's not hard; it just takes commitment to attend.

These events typically run for two or three days. I make sure that as soon as I return, I take the time to disseminate the information I've gathered to my team and clients. This, too, is important; there's no value in you running in the front door after you've been away on a perceived junket, jumping around the room like someone is chasing you with a cattle prod and telling your team that you're about to change the world because you've just come up with a telepathic version of Viagra. All you'll get with that approach is blank stares and the mumbling of, "Oh man, here we go again. He'll get back to normal in a few days when the Kool-Aid wears off."

The information you have gathered is, of course, important. Don't discount that for one minute. Just keep in mind that you were there and your team members were not. Recreating for them the same buzz you received when you had the light bulb go off will take some thought and consideration as to how you will construct your communication to them.

Set Yourself a Course

What course can you enroll in each year? Learning opportunities come in many forms—some structured, some unstructured. The structured component of your information gathering will offer you discipline and consistency. Maybe it's a language you'll learn, or a particular discipline of business you'll master, or a personal development course that might just bring more perspective or balance to your life. You don't have to take a difficult or long course; in fact, it doesn't even have to be a business course. Just something that gives you another tick in the information box.

Write It Down

If you're anything like me, then you've got a brain like a computer. It has a limited hard drive that can't hold too much information, and an auto delete button that gets rid of the old stuff and then dutifully crashes. The only way for me to counter this process is to write things down—particularly items on which I need to take action.

Years ago, I was working at a radio station under a very smart station manager. Every Friday night we'd head to the boardroom for a couple of quick drinks after work. These quick drinks would often turn into a session that ran until the refrigerator was empty and staff was wringing the necks of bottles trying to get the last drop of free booze out of them. During each one of these sessions, our station manager would intently ask questions of all of us as he mingled with the crowd. Then, come Monday morning, he'd inevitably come to our desks and say, "Hey, you know what you were talking about on Friday night? I'd like to talk more about that when you have time today." This usually prompted an internal voice to start screaming, "What did I say, what did I do! . . . and did anyone take pictures?" Our brains would race to replay the night's events in fast-forward, while we searched through the scattered memories for some kind of assurance that we didn't do anything truly humiliating or potentially illegal in more than one country.

I can recall countless occasions on which I simply stared blankly at him with no idea of what I had said the previous Friday night, thinking the whole time, "I'm sure he was as hammered as I was; how did he remember that?" I usually followed his question with some lame, generic statement in an effort to recall some part of the conversation. "Yeah, well, I just wanted to let you know how I felt about that. What was your key takeaway from our discussion?" If I was lucky, he'd take the bait and launch back into the conversation as though we were still having it. This would provide my mind with an extra few seconds to find the pieces of the puzzle through the booze haze and pull it together—which was sometimes followed by an internal sigh of "Yes, that's it. *That*'s what he's talking about; thank God for that. I finally remembered."

It was some time before I learned of my boss's trick: During the course of the evening's events, he would quietly step out of the room from time to time and make notes on conversations to avoid forgetting the sometimes-important information he was gathering from staff. Clever! It was an amazing lesson he taught me, without even knowing he was a teacher.

Ever since then, I've made sure that when potentially important or interesting information comes my way, I'll stop and either punch a note into my phone, write it on a business card, send myself a voice message, or find another way to store it so I don't forget. Even more importantly, I'm careful not to forget the *interpretation* of the information I have gathered.

Recently, my old radio boss and his wonderful wife came to visit us in Florida. And I must admit, I took extreme delight in keeping him up until 2 A.M., drinking beers and wine and speaking in a language that was a mix of Australian, American, and a bit of Balkan thrown in for good measure, making certain that we really couldn't understand each other. As he used to do all those years ago, I slipped out of the room from time to time, and I wrote down some notes. This made our breakfast conversation so much sweeter for me. At last, I was able to look into *his* bleary eyes and see him think, "Were we really talking about that last night?" I had my revenge! We had a great laugh when I let on that I worked out what he was doing all those years ago during our Friday night drinks and that I'd been applying the lesson I learned from him ever since. We had come full circle.

Information comes in so many forms; your consciousness to be continually gathering it *today* will set your competitive platform of the *future*.

Real Information!

Three things you need to do now to Future-Proof Your Business and make sure you are gathering real information.

Action One

Sometimes we think we are absorbing information, but are we really taking it in? Think back to the last two books you read, the last two conferences you traveled to, and the last two networking events you attended. How much of the information you absorbed have you really taken onboard and put into action in your business? Make a rule moving forward to seek to change one thing a day.

Action Two

Do you really show a genuine unrequited interest in others, or are your attempts at networking all about you? The next time you're in a networking environment, try to focus solely on serving and helping others. Make it about them and not about you.

Action Three

Do you have a real desire to absorb information, or do you just pay lip service to the concept? What strategy do you use to ensure that you are taking in information deliberately and specifically to assist you in life? You've heard the saying that you learn something new every day—so put that into practice. Ask yourself at the end of each day: "What did I learn today?"

CHAPTER 8

Strategy that Sticks

"I learned that just because you write your strategy down it does not make you any smarter, it does not make it real, nor does it mean it's a good 'strategy.'"

I can remember my very first business plan. I had put together a document to present to the bank in an attempt to raise $1.2 million to buy a regional radio station that was for sale. It was a big ask, really—particularly given the fact that I was only 26 years old. I'd raised about $500,000 from family and friends and needed the balance of funds from the bank. I read books, spoke to business mentors, bought all sorts of business tools, and borrowed business plans from anyone I could. Armed with this information, I proceeded to put together the greatest lot of total rubbish I have ever put on paper in my entire life.

And, to my amazement—it *worked.*

I still recall leaving the bank and thinking to myself, "I just might actually own a radio station by Monday ... and I have no idea what I am doing!" Over the few days that followed, I felt a mixture of excitement and total terror at the thought of what was looming before me.

As it turned out, we lost the deal at the 11th hour; another cash bidder stole it from under us. It was simply not to be. And I must say, looking back, I'm glad it turned out that way because I reckon it could have been a disaster. The experience did teach me something, however: Just because you write your strategy down, it does not make you any smarter, does not make it real, and does not mean it's a good "strategy." And it doesn't mean that what you've written will actually come true. In my first plan, I had written a bunch of glowing material about our team, the money we would make out of the business, the bright future of radio, and how quickly I could pay back the bank. But the big problem with this was that even I was not sure *I* believed it myself.

The simple reason that we were finally able to get the money we needed was *not* because I could achieve all the things I wrote in the plan I presented. It was because the bloke who lent me the money simply did not know very much about running a radio station either, but he wanted it to work just as badly as I did. Think about it: He turns out to be the guy who funds this bright young entrepreneur into a wonderful success story. *Wow*, that would look good on his resume!

In short, I sold both him *and* me on the concept. In fact, I managed to talk both of us into it in one go.

It was not so much that I was lying to him. I just didn't know any better and was starting to believe my own story. The sum of my research to put the deal together was my years of experience as a radio station employee. Sure, I was in management, but I'd never really put myself on the line for the business. I had not done much due diligence on the industry, nor did I really understand the asset I was buying. I just *wanted* it. So passion and enthusiasm got in the way of preparation, research, and good judgment.

Unfortunately, the one quality I lacked that is absolutely core to good strategy was objectivity.

So, lesson one of building a good strategy is to do your homework. Ask yourself these questions as you gather information, before you even start writing a strategy. And make sure you are answering objectively—and *truthfully*.

- What have you done to research your business or your business concept?
- What are the facts surrounding the business you are dealing with?
- Are you really looking at your business with truth and reality, or are you all blue skies and BS?
- Have you surrounded yourself with peers, consultants, mentors, and others who can help you remain objective, gather information, and conduct research?
- Are your financial forecasts conservative?
- Are you using historical patterns and trends to assist you in figuring out the future?
- Have you done your due diligence when forming or acquiring a new company—and have you done it *objectively*? It's very easy to fall in love with an idea or an asset. But remember, this kind of love can wear off very quickly.

Conducting research puts you in a much stronger position to begin developing your strategy.

So, what's next? Well, first of all, there is absolutely *no* value in writing something that you are never going to read again. Business plans and strategy documents should be used as reference documents; they are meant to keep your business on an even keel and your mind focused. So, that being the case, make the document something that is easy for you to use and read, something that's written in your personal style. Don't make it 200 pages long if that is going to keep you from accessing content that's too hard to find, too wordy, or too full of rhetorical statements that nobody cares about. On the other hand, don't make it so short that you can't remember what you were talking about in the bullet points you've written down. Don't cram it full of terms, acronyms, and jargon that a third party can't understand or interpret; that, too, will render it useless as a reference for others.

My business strategy documents today are centered on information and action. I split them into an executive overview and five key business drivers:

1. Business strategy
2. Operations strategy
3. Human relations/people strategy
4. Financial strategy
5. Marketing strategy

Each section contains a written introduction of a few paragraphs to explain the things we need to address in that business driver. Following the introduction page, there is an action grid that outlines the items we need to address. This helps us clearly understand what we need to do in order for us to fulfill the objectives we set out in the corresponding introduction, and it allows us to tick the issues off as the year goes by. It also gives us an easy reference point for each of our monthly administration strategy summits, quarterly business planning strategy summits, and twice-yearly strategy retreats.

Figure 8.1 shows what our action grid looks like.

Issue	Focus	Objective	Action	Outcome	Who	When
We number issues for reference as there may be a number of things to take action on related to the same issue.	What is the core matter we're addressing with this part of the strategy? Give the issue a title as a reference.	What are we trying to achieve by addressing this particular issue?	What core action do we have to take to make a change and address this issue?	What is the desired outcome we are seeking by addressing this issue in the business?	Who is going to be responsible for making this change in the business?	When are we going to have this complete? (This may include progress milestones along the way to completion.)

Figure 8.1   Strategic Plan Action Grid

Typically, the items in the action grid are color-coded, with each color assigned a different meaning relative to where they are in the execution of that particular project. This way, we're able to see how we are doing at a glance; here's an example of how you might do that.

- **Black**: Yet to be addressed. These are items we'll be taking care of in six months' time or more; in other words, two quarters.
- **Blue**: Unfinished strategy issue to be reviewed next quarter.
- **Green**: Completed on schedule.
- **Yellow**: Already in progress and on target at this time for completion this quarter.
- **Red**: Behind schedule.

Following are the types of matters we address in regard to each of the business drivers.

Executive Overview

Our strategic philosophy with this business driver is "short, sharp, and real." This is typically a one- or two-page summary of the overall business strategy and our core plan for the next 12 months. The summary covers the key topics on which we need to focus to achieve our business objectives and, in turn, our business vision.

The executive overview also summarizes each of the business drivers' milestones for the year. It provides a line or two on the critical items for each driver, and how we expect that issue to impact the overall business. I typically carry this around with me in my folio as a quick reference if something pops up for which I need a memory jolt. This is my one-page, microwave strategic planning document.

Business Strategy Overview

Our strategic philosophy with this business driver is "deep and deliberate."

This is the core strategy for the overall plan, the big picture stuff we need to address. It may include topics such as a change in business positioning, new product development, mergers and acquisitions, expansion, and other matters that influence the business from a helicopter view.

This part of the strategy involves a discussion of the complete business vision and how the actions we are taking this year will affect our efforts to achieve that vision. We also nominate key objectives for the year, a handful of items that we've deemed as the most important focal points for the business.

Operations Strategy

Our strategic philosophy with this business driver is "change or die."

This section focuses on business efficiencies and the day-to-day company operations. This is where we talk about the things we will do to improve our procedures as the business grows or changes. This driver is all about change, and not just making change an action but a consciousness as well. We drill into individuals' roles and responsibilities in relation to the operation of the business and link those to performance indicators relative to those individuals. With this in place, we're in a position to work on our human relations or people strategy.

Human Relations/People Strategy

Our strategic philosophy with this business driver is "right person right place." As the years have gone by, I have changed my philosophy on staff selection. Instead of just filling a role with a person, I now focus more intently on finding the right person and then fitting that individual into a role that is suitable to them, and their future in the business.

Our people plan is critical to the success of the overall strategy. If team members have not bought into the vision and direction for the year, then the rest of the plan is, in short, screwed. This section of the strategy outlines how we manage and reward staff, set key performance indicators (KPIs), and allocate responsibility for projects from the strategy. We also use it to review our profit-sharing program for the company and decide what is fair for all.

The next thing we do is outline resource needs for the year. Do we need more people, fewer people, or the same people to execute the plan? We'll also cover the issue of the external contractors that we use from time to time. We will consider their performance throughout the previous year and set them some guidelines for the year to come.

A key to this part of the strategy is to involve all staff members in the conversations that surround its development. I rarely set goals and KPIs for them; instead, I encourage them to set their own milestones in relation to the overall business strategy. We do this through team workshops and one-on-one conversations. This way, everyone has buy in, and everyone is clear, and I'm not the big bad wolf that snaps at everyone's heels each day to get them to work harder.

Financial Strategy

When it comes to a financial strategy, we adopt the strategic philosophy of "first what, then how." We figure out *what* resource we need to grow the business to shift it in the strategic direction we want in the future. We then determine *how* we are going to find and secure the money to do that—well before we need it.

In my early days in business, I often found myself getting caught mid-financial year, scratching around for cash for a last-minute asset, resource, or piece of equipment we needed that was critical to achieving our annual goals. Now we look to anticipate the things we *might* need for the year and set about finding the money for those items *now*!

Of course, we cover the obvious elements of cash flow, profit and loss, debtors, creditors, and the policies surrounding those items. But the biggest element of our financial strategy is to do something that I call "future-izing" the business to prepare financially for the things we cannot see just yet.

The best time to ask for money from someone is when you don't need it. I have frequently found myself in a conversation with someone who is heading to the bank the next day to ask for an overdraft extension due to the fact that business "is not going too well," or he "didn't anticipate [insert unexpected event] happening." Because I can see the fear in their eyes as they tell me their stories, chances are that their bankers will, too, and that's why they *won't* get the money. Too little, too late . . . too bad.

Marketing Strategy

Our strategic philosophy with this business driver is

"Perception is reality." We're very clear that the way we want our clients to perceive us to be is the way we *are*.

For this reason, we spread our marketing message over a number of levels to ensure that they're receiving the right message and company positioning.

To give us a solid, integrated approach to our marketing, our strategy is broken down into these levels:

1. Brand strategy
2. Area strategy
3. Relationship strategy
4. Local strategy
5. Information technology strategy
6. Training strategy

In Chapter 11, I provide an overview of the entire plan and then drill down into its tactical execution on each level. This is critical to the company's development, because nothing happens in business until you make a sale.

You can have the best systems, processes, and back-of-house setup, but without customers and sales, nobody will ever see them.

So, how do we pull all of these strategic elements together?

Every January, at our half-yearly retreat, we do a total overhaul of the strategic plan. This includes a discussion about how the previous year's plan went compared to what we had planned and written down. And then we give ourselves a completely honest and thorough overall rating on our performance.

Our planning sessions always take at least two days; we don't cut any corners. The objective is to write a document with meaning and outcomes so we are all clear on what we are trying to achieve both as a business and as individuals.

Everything we do as a business is an open book. We make all elements of the strategy visible for all team members to view—right down to the profit and loss statements and even my salary. (I heard you gasp when you read that!) A transparent strategy brings clarity to your vision of the future.

Real Strategy!

Three things you need to do now to Future-Proof Your Business and make sure you really have great strategy that sticks.

Action One

Don't just write a plan; write one that you are actually going to read and refer to!

Action Two

Share the plan with *everyone* who has a stake in it—your spouse, your staff, your advisors, anyone who has a significant influence on the day-to-day management of your business.

Action Three

Review the plan regularly. This should be a living document that you adjust and change to suit the market influencers and things that impact your business throughout the year.

CHAPTER

9

The Rewards of Rewards

"The first lesson for me was to stop thinking like a leader and business owner and start remembering what it was like to be a staff member myself."

With vision and strategy in place and a clear understanding of your position as a leader, you've established a great platform for the way you develop real and meaningful relationships with your team. Now it's time to work out how to have them help you guide the business into the future.

Over the years, I've had the chance to lead a number of great teams of people. One of the most significant lessons I've learned was that even after I was able to lead these individuals properly, my job of keeping them engaged was *far* from done. The next cornerstone to getting the most from them in the workplace was to introduce some kind of reward.

Ten years ago, it was perfectly acceptable to say things like, "I pay my staff, so I expect a fair day's work out of them in return." Nowadays, that just doesn't wash—particularly when you are working with members of Generation Y.

It took me many years of trial and error before I got a workable, manageable, and believable staff reward system in place in our companies. And even *then* I wasn't sure if it was right. However, it was the best we could come up with. The cornerstone of my success with this approach was for me to openly and honestly share everything about the business with the employees.

The following are some of the highs, lows, and total screwups I had in my journey to create a meaningful rewards program with my teams.

Failure Number One: Rewards for Rewards' Sake

My first reward program was sheer rocket science. Okay, okay, so maybe not. Actually, you would have probably thought the only way I could have come up with it was that I was dropped on my head at birth.

The fact was that you couldn't really call it a program, since there really *wasn't* one.

I'd simply pay our employees a random amount of money (dependent on what I had left over in the bank) around Christmas time, because, well—that's just what you do, right? You walk around the office acting like Santa with your chest puffed out thinking you are doing the right thing handing out cash left and right. Then you retreat to your office and wait for the wonderful thank-you notes to be left for you, along with offers to fetch you a cup of coffee every other minute.

Then a few days pass without any kind of acknowledgment. Nobody says anything to you about the wonderful Christmas bonus, and you simply think that all staff members are an ungrateful waste of space. You dwell on how "this would be a great business if I didn't have to employ those bloodsuckers out in front." You think about how you should have just gone and burned the cash on the Christmas barbecue with mates to at least have a more real and meaningful experience of the smell of money going up in smoke.

Ah, yes, I am sure there has been a moment that we've all said something like that *sometime* in our leadership lifetimes.

However, the *real* reason nobody cared about the random Christmas bonuses was that there was no program in place. No system let them know how much they were to be rewarded or provided any kind of metrics outlining what they needed to achieve through the year in order to qualify for the payment. So of course, what you gave them was never enough for what they felt they had done throughout the year. All my employees saw was me throwing a few bucks around, and then going away someplace nice for the Christmas holidays—packing up my desk and leaving them behind to mind the fort as I disappeared in a puff of dust kicked up by my new Range Rover.

Not a good look for *any* boss.

Failure Number Two: You Screw Up, You Sort It Out

This one was a classic. It occurred when the time came to conduct staff salary reviews—and I overpaid all of them. I somehow figured, using the amazing "Troy logic" that exists somewhere in my brain, that this then gave me the right to say to them: "You're paid a salary. If you screw up, then you need to find a way to pay for your screwups."

Utterly ridiculous!

In other words, I argued that because they were now being paid so well, I could charge them with the financial responsibility of fixing their own mistakes. By way of example: If they made a decision that cost us $2,000 off the bottom line, then they had to come to me with a plan for how they were going to recover it—or it would affect their next bonus review.

The outcome of this approach was that my staff members spent most of their day in fear of screwing up, and as a result, avoided taking risks and thinking laterally. Nor would they step outside a safe zone of productivity, for fear of erring in a way that would cost money that they'd then have to find a way to recover. In other words, they came to work each day afraid of making a mistake.

I was totally using fear-based management methods that were causing negative energy in the workplace, which in turn made my staff more likely to make mistakes. It did not inspire anyone to try harder; instead, they were looking to place blame. I also found myself constantly asking, "So, how are you going to fix that?" None of us was claiming responsibility for *anything*.

Failure Number Three: Prove You're Not a Screwup

My next attempt was *almost* equally as stupid. But at least this one had a system. I think.

With another flash of brilliance, I called a meeting in the boardroom one January day. I had charged into the office telling everyone there to "Stop what you're doing! I have a great plan for you for this year, and I want to share it with you straightaway." The minions excitedly and dutifully followed me into the room, pens and pads in hand. They sat with bated breath like a young woman at a restaurant as she waits in anticipation for her beau to pop the magical question that will set her on a path of bliss for the rest of her life.

Again, you could hear the crickets in the background. But this time, I had them. And I could *feel it*.

The system was simple. I handed all my employees notes informing them that I had put a sum of money into individual personal accounts on their behalf. The key was that while they could see the money, they were not able to access it until the end of the year. They were kind of like a bunch of confused babies in a topless bar—so much to have, but just not quite sure how to go about getting it.

Oh. Well. Yes. Of course, there was a catch.

I went on to explain to them that while that was their bonus for the year—paid in advance—I would chisel some of that money away every time they made a mistake in the business that was clearly due to their incompetence, stupidity, or simple bad decision. Wow, what an inspiration!

As you can imagine, as the year wore on and mistakes were made, morale started to dip. However, it wasn't enough that they knew *instinctively* that they had cost themselves some money when they messed up. Oh no—I had to point that out to them and publicly embarrass them in front of their peers. Yeah, *that* would show them! Let's get them all naked in front of their mates while I stayed fully clothed at the head of the boardroom table. I figured they would learn from each others' mistakes.

Each quarter at our business planning strategy summits, I would reel off the names of those who had cost us money and describe the impact this would have on their bonuses. And each quarter, they could see their diminishing Christmas cheer; and each quarter, they become less and less engaged—not only in the program but in the company as a whole. Oh yeah, brilliant plan on my part. And, as expected by all, there was not much left in their accounts by the end of the year. And I went from being Santa Claus to the Grinch.

What an amazing way to motivate someone. Give something to them and then slowly and painfully—*and* in front of their peers—take it *back* from them.

These mistakes seem so incredibly dumb when I look back on them. Yet having worked as a business consultant for so many years now, it's interesting to see just how many business leaders take exactly the same, foolish approach with their staff reward programs. For some reason, they are just not willing to treat employees with trust and respect like equal human beings. So, of course, they get zero trust or respect back from those they are trying to engage.

Fortunately for me, I made all of these mistakes early in my business career. I blamed a lot of my shortcomings on a lack of maturity, given that I started in business when I was only 26. The balance of the problem was my ego and my fear of asking someone to help me to get it right.

The first lesson for me was to stop thinking like a leader and business owner, and start remembering what it was like to be a staff member myself. I had to recall all of the things that inspired me to work a bit harder in the business as well as all of the things that used to really annoy me about the boss.

Semi-Success Number One: We'll Reward You ... I Think

So I took myself away at Christmas break. I sat on a beach and attempted to figure out how I could do a better job of inspiring and engaging my teams.

Step one was to put key performance indicators (KPIs) in place. So I developed metrics to see how everyone was actually doing in relation to productivity.

This was a good start, especially since it gave me the chance to look at my own KPIs. We attached these to our activity logs, and all of a sudden we had a time effectiveness tool in place. Good start.

Then I sat down and worked out everyone's "cost of seat." In other words, I wanted see exactly how much each of my staff members cost me per hour/week/month/year. So we worked out a simple formula:

- Total cost of an individual's salary + extras (superannuation/holiday loading/average sick days) = $X
- Add the individual's share of the overhead (a basic formula of total cost of overhead, less salaries, divided by the number of employees in the business) = $Y

- Then I added the two together: $X + Y = Z$ = annual cost of seat for that individual
- Divide Z by 1,920 hours (the total number of hours I estimated they could work in a year based on an average 40-hour workweek, minus their holidays/public holidays/ average sick days = about 48 weeks)
- Equals cost of seat on an hourly basis: H
- Final formula: $X + Y = Z \div 1,920 = H$

This did two things for me: It gave me cost of productivity and helped me understand when I was (and was not) making money on a project. It also revealed the gap between what we quoted versus how long we actually took to execute and what that cost us as well.

Now that I had this information, I figured we *had* to turn a profit—because I was completely clear on what everyone was costing me. Now I could work back from this and come up with a revenue number we had to hit for the year if we were to be as effective as we could be. In other words, each of us would be getting the most out of our 1,920 hours a year at work.

Where this all came undone was when I realized that although this system was great *theoretically*, it was tough to put into practice.

First of all, I knew that we weren't going to work all of the 1,920 hours in a year. However, I assumed we might be able to work 70 percent of them. This was then my real cost (RC), and now my formula looked something like this.

$$X + Y = Z \div 1,920 = H \div 70\% = RC$$

So, why was this formula not as significant as $e = MC^2$?

Merely coming up with the number did not automatically allow us to charge the clients more due to the fact that we were not being time-effective. In fact, all it did was show the team how much time they were wasting—and all *this* did was cause them to become more frustrated with the overruns on projects we had quoted.

One good thing that came out of this was that we got a *great* KPI metric. For the first time, we could see how much we were making or losing on a project, right down to the hour.

Sounds good, right?

Except there was a flaw in creating the reward system. Our simple math revealed that throughout the course of the year, in at least one of our companies, more than $4 million worth of client business was not profitable. And, in fact, these clients represented 60 percent of revenue. Oops!

So while the employees were all initially excited about hitting their KPIs and getting their bonuses at the beginning of the year, we began to realize that we were, in fact, working for *nothing* more than 60 percent of the time. The sales and profit targets seemed far too distant, and motivation started to drop. It was clear we were not going to hit our KPIs based on the fact that we'd set our productivity hurdles too high and our margins were still too low. The scales were just not balanced.

I was busy chasing new business wherever I could find it. However, as soon as we started working with some of our new clients, it became obvious that some of these projects were clearly not going to hit our productivity or profit targets. Yet we still took these clients on, as in some instances we needed them just for the cash flow and turnover. It's one thing to say you only want profitable clients, but when you've identified that more than half of your clients are not, and you're trying to reorganize 60 percent of your client roster to make them profitable or exchange them for profitable clients, managing that cash flow impact becomes a little more tricky.

So really, in some instances I was just making it harder for the staff to hit targets by failing to recognize my own profit and productivity metrics when I was going through the process of client selection. Every day I was making tough decisions: take the cash with the potentially bad client and stress the team, or pass on the client and potentially place a cash flow stress on the business.

Despite their efforts to work harder and faster, the team was losing sight of how they were going to be rewarded for it. Over the course of the year, we eventually did re-sign the unprofitable clients; however, we didn't replace the volume fast enough for staff to achieve their productivity and profit KPIs and, in turn, their bonuses. While we *were* more profitable on a project basis, there was no knock-on effect on the team financially as lost volume affected our overall profit performance.

In short, we were using the wrong metrics and operating under the wrong program!

I finally figured out that we were only watching the top line revenue versus hours to execute projects. Productivity was only one metric when it came to expenses and profit.

So, it was back to the drawing board.

Success Number One: True Reward Comes When It's Transparent

After another two years of getting the reward program wrong in our companies, I figured that the only way to get it right—and introduce a system that the team believed in—was for me to be *totally* transparent with them and reveal everything. Otherwise, any KPI I designed to measure their performance could have been tampered with or perceived to have been engineered so that they worked harder without the corresponding rewards.

So at our half-yearly strategy retreat, I announced the following: "The next thing on the agenda is the staff incentive and reward program." This was met with the usual sighs, groans, and nods of "Yeah, but we try this every year, and every year, it just doesn't work."

At that moment, I handed each of the team a copy of last year's profit and loss and balance sheet statements. The only thing I stripped out was the staff salaries, which I put into one line item, so they had some privacy among their peers as to what they were being paid. My salary was shown as the second staff salaries line; it was out there, bare to the world, bold as brass for all to see.

As soon as they noticed that I was not only showing them how the company was doing, line item by line item, but also what I was personally making out of the business, they turned and looked at me with bewildered and somewhat curious expressions.

I grinned and went on.

"Okay—if we are to come up with something that gets you guys out of bed every morning, then we need to be a bit more lateral and a lot more transparent as to how the business is going. I need to show you the raw truth. This is now your business as much as it is mine, and that's how I am going to reward you from here on in. Otherwise, this is never going to work for any of us."

And so the new program began. Step one was for us to all sign off on what we felt we could achieve for the year, revenue-wise. We did a month-by-month analysis of every current and potential client and the projects we had for each. Once we set some real numbers against these, everyone signed off on the total revenue number for the year. This no longer entailed me slapping the table, giving the "go team go!" speech and informing my team what we would do that year in revenue. It was now their job to say, "Here's what we feel we can realistically do this year in revenue by working diligently but without killing ourselves—and we are all happy with that."

Then we went through the expenses line by line and negotiated each of the items to see if the numbers needed to increase or decrease—and one of these items happened to be my salary. I left the room for 30 minutes while the team negotiated what they felt I should be paid for the year relative to my financial exposure, my investment in the business, and my lifestyle.

This step was vital to the process. If I was to reward my staff based on profit, then I didn't want them to think that I was taking unnecessary cash out of the business in a salary or in any other way that could interfere with them achieving those profit numbers. And anyway, I've always been a pretty simple bloke; even today, give me holidays with my beautiful wife, a fast car on a race track, a good bottle of wine over lunch with my mates, and a water view, and I'm happy.

When the expenses were agreed upon and signed off on, we then determined how everyone should be rewarded for our success and profitability. After about two hours of discussion, the incentive formula looked something like this:

- Total $ revenue for the year = $X
- Less total $ expenses for the year = $Y
- Equals total Earnings Before Interest and Tax (EBIT) = $Z

For every dollar achieved over and above the agreed target, the staff received 50 cents pretax of that dollar as an incentive bonus.

The post-tax profit was distributed to shareholders—as per our shareholder agreement—with 30 percent distribution to shareholders, 40 percent in retained earnings, and 30 percent invested in capital expenditure. This also showed the team that we would give them the working capital and the tools they needed throughout the year to help them hit their targets.

However, there were a few rules relative to the distribution that I let the employees create themselves. After all, this was their system, not mine.

- The financial distribution is shared equally among all staff.
- Each staff member would continue to have an individual salary review for the year. The expense budget also accounted for this indicative salary review allocation before sign-off.
- Staff must be part of the team for at least six months to qualify for the incentive scheme.

- Staff members who leave before the end of the financial year forfeit their incentive entitlements.
- Staff who work part-time receive pro rata distribution of the incentive entitlement.

But this reward was in no way a handout. Employees only received money if their KPIs were met, and we designated those parameters in the following way:

- KPIs existed on three levels. This not only tied the departments in the company together, but it also united the staff within those departments, thereby improving team spirit.
- Individual staff members must achieve 100 percent of their KPIs.
- Their departmental teams must achieve 100 percent of the team KPIs in order to fulfill their overall percentage of their teams' responsibility for the company targets. Each team takes equal responsibility in the overall company KPI.
- The overall company KPIs determine what percentage of distributions *all* staff members receive. If they hit 100 percent of the company's KPIs, then they receive 100 percent of their bonus incentive; if they hit 90 percent, they receive 90 percent of their bonus incentive, and so on.
- Bonuses are calculated and paid within 90 days of the end of the financial year.

This way, staff members pushed themselves to get their individual percentages up; team members pushed each other to reach the team KPIs; and teams encouraged one another to achieve 100 percent of the company KPIs. In essence, they are all handcuffed together, and the program made them accountable for each other's success.

The system is summarized in Figure 9.1.

Each staff member's KPI sheet looked like a simple score-card on which we tried to put all relevant information for ease of referral. The sheet was split into key drivers that included customer service, business development, project management, and personal development to maintain a sense of balance in their day.

Figure 9.2 shows an example of how we worked out our key performance indicators.

While this system's total transparency and honesty worked very well, I quickly realized during the first year of its

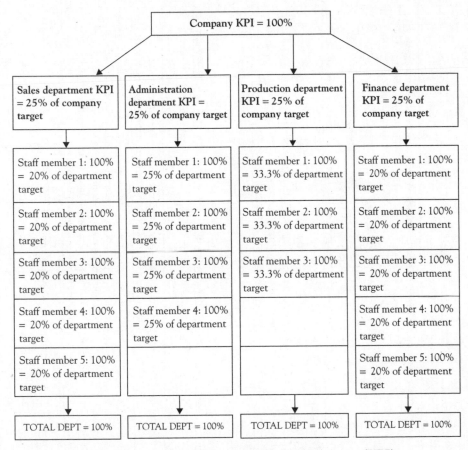

Figure 9.1 **Personal Key Performance Indicators (KPI)**

KPI	TARGET	BY WHEN	WEIGHT
Project Management	• Deliver 100% required project outcomes in accordance with agreed production milestones set out and agreed with clients contracts. • Provide daily project updates in morning 'Charlie' calls. • Provide weekly project updates at staff Administration meeting. • Provide client contact reports from all meetings and log into intranet. • Provide monthly client call reports. • Keep daily diary / activity logs and present to directors monthly.	Ongoing	30%
Client Management	• Same day telephone call back. • Same day email return (unless off premises). • Review all personal clients on the data base to establish their validity for the quarterly mail out. • Assume all client project responsibility for allocated clients.		25%
New Business Networking	• Attend two networking functions per quarter (breakfast / business learning event / lunch / industry networking event / business group meeting). • Make 2 referral or new business calls per month to build your network. • Contribute to the quarterly Business Planning Strategy Summit meeting.	Ongoing	15%
Marketing / Business Development Research	• Research 12 ideas per annum for contribution to the marketing pool. • Research 12 ideas per annum for possible business development activity.	Update monthly	15%
Competitor Research	• Provide quarterly updates to the competitor spreadsheet on one competitor in the category at the Business Planning Strategy Summit.	Quarterly Business Planning Strategy Summit	5%
Personal Development	• Attend 1 company-funded business-related course, your choice. (You will be required to put forward a business case on how this will add value to your role in the company, or improve you as a business person.) • Complete your personal vision and plan by December 30th and provide updates on this at quarterly KPI reviews.	By Next 2 Day Strategy Retreat	10%

Figure 9.2   Key Performance Indicators

128

implementation that there was one more modification I needed to make to keep the momentum going. We had to provide employees with more specific updates on how they were doing throughout the year. A running scorecard like this would show them more regular KPIs in relation to the budgets we'd set, which meant that all staff could calculate a potential outcome for the end of the financial year as the year went on, and work toward improving that outcome each quarter. A one-page summary did the job; the sheet simply showed money in, money out, profit, and personal and team KPI performance.

In addition to the annual bonus, I introduced quarterly rewards for achieving targets. We would sit down each quarter for our business planning strategy summits to run the numbers, review the last quarter, and forecast the coming quarter. If the profit target for the quarter had been met, we'd all head out for the afternoon off and some fun. If not, we'd head back to work for the afternoon . . . and then still head for a beer at five o'clock to drink like fourteenth-century pirates and bury the result from the last quarter in booze. Either way, we'd all be on deck the next day for a fresh (though somewhat blurry) start to a new quarter and a new opportunity to meet targets and receive the next quarter's reward.

Last but not least on the list of rewards was Christmas. This one was easy for me. Given the fact that I had a team of females, there is only one reward that makes sense at Christmas: the little blue box from Tiffany's.

The lesson on rewards was not an easy one to learn. The key was to have the team always learning from the result of the *past*, so they may improve their personal position in the *future*.

Once you get it right, your team will have much better flow and connection—particularly if you figure a way to handcuff their goals and rewards together. This system also allowed me to get out of the office and develop the business. As an example, in one of our best and most profitable financial years, I spent 240 days *out* of the office. The reason we had such a great year without my help? Easy! It was not my money they were making or losing—it was *theirs*!

Real Rewards!

Three things you need to do now to Future-Proof Your Business and make sure you are offering real rewards.

Action One

Does your staff incentive program actually provide incentive? Or are you offering a cop-out because you're, well, cheap? In other words, would *you* be excited about your incentive program if *you* were the employee?

Action Two

Do your KPIs actually act as indicators, or are they just numbers on a page to make everyone feel good? And who created them—you or you *and* your staff in an effort to get everyone to buy in to the system?

Action Three

Are you engaging your staff in the process or dictating the outcome? Is this what you *all* want to see out of the business? That's how you provide a real incentive to achieve both everyone's personal vision and the business vision.

CHAPTER 10

Show Me the Money

*"The key to taking the cash flow stress out of growth was to try
and be more of a conduit between my vendors and my clients."*

Business and money. The two are inextricably linked; yet
we do everything we can to separate them. In my lesson
on strategy I gave a brief explanation of my financial
planning philosophy: "First what, then how."

Now that you've had a bit of a reality check on the strategic
positioning of the business, let me explain in a little more detail
exactly *why* this is my philosophy.

Now, I need to be clear: I am not a financial planner, nor
an accountant—nor do I hold myself out to be either. In truth,
I am pretty crappy with the detail of numbers. I think back to
my days at school when I used to sell condoms for $1 each to
my fellow students. I remember that I could do the numbers
in my head and figure that I was making a profit, but I was
never very good at honing in on the details.

> It's usually not until someone begins to lose money in business that you determine how to get the most out of the money you do have.

The following describes some of my good days and my bad days and my lessons on money.

Any form of growth in business—in products, people, planning, promotion, or business preparation—costs money. And the easiest way to accommodate that cost is to plan for it.

It took the experience of running five companies before I was able to slap some sense into myself and stop trying to convince myself—and others—that growth would not need investment and that I could bootstrap it out of cash flow and sales. Now, I know many of you would have grown and developed your businesses out of pure cash flow, and I know you are probably very proud of that, as I am. But be honest with me: Some of those days were nothing short of seriously hard work. How many times have you bet the house on a deal or put staff salaries on your credit card?

In my early years, I realized that a lot of the stress of this method of managing cash comes from not being in control of your financial destiny. Many times I would do a deal or take on a new client, knowing full well that it was going to cost me money to fund that new business. I just figured that if we invoiced them on time and they paid within our terms, then the moon and the stars would align and the world would be a beautiful place.

And that was my first mistake. I would have had a better chance of having Elvis sing nude at our company Christmas party than having all of our invoices paid on time.

What I couldn't seem to understand was that the new client I'd just brought on board was probably doing the same thing in *his* business: hoping that all would fall into place on time with *his* new clients. And his new clients were probably doing the same thing with *their* new clients; and so the dominoes get stacked. Something goes pear-shaped with a deal four degrees of separation away from my business, and the dominoes start to fall. One client's client is late paying him, and so *my* new client is late paying me, and then before I know it, I'm in arrears with my creditors and the good money fairy gets swatted by the evil debt devil. All of a sudden, we're in a financial hole that resembles the national debt.

Sure, we have a new client, but we've got no money in the bank, and, because nobody is paying their bills, we're going out the back door faster than a rat up a drainpipe. Take on two more clients and my problem compounds. The further you are separated from the source of the money, the longer you wait to be paid—and the worse the cash flow crunch gets.

The answer here was not for us to stop growing; we just needed to plan more thoroughly and realistically for that growth.

The lesson we learned here was to *always* plan for the worst. If an account was issued with a 7-day payment term, we'd bank on seeing the money in 90 days. Of course we were going to chase it, but we couldn't just *hope* everything would go well and that our clients would do exactly what they promised to do. We had to be in control of our own financial destiny.

The second mistake I made was to assume that I could use my creditors as bankers to get me out of a cash flow hole.

Bankers will often encourage businesses to hit up their suppliers and creditors for better terms—to effectively use *them* as a bank. After all, the bank's credit rating relates in part to its ability to pay on call, which essentially equals *your* ability to pay on call. Remember that your banker is in business just like you. The bank has the same issues to deal with their own cash flow and debt-to-equity ratio balance to keep in check. It is just a bigger, uglier animal. But the bank can still go broke just as fast as the next guy; 2008 proved that. Asking you to hit up your suppliers for better terms and use them as an overdraft simply shifts the risk for your bank to your vendors. Think about it: Why would your suppliers be okay with you sticking it to them for extended payment, better terms, payment plans, consignment stock, or some sort of deal to make *your* life easier and theirs harder? It just doesn't make business (or common) sense. And it certainly does not make for great relationships in the future.

I am not for one minute saying you shouldn't negotiate with your suppliers and creditors for a deal. But don't keep going back to them and beating the last breath out of them just to help you out of a financial hole you've put yourself in. These guys are not dumb; they know where you're at just by watching the way you conduct your business. And if you *are* dealing with a cash flow issue in your business, be honest with those who need to know about it. You'll be surprised just how much support honesty will bring. I've found that the key to taking the cash flow stress out of growth is to act as more of a conduit between my suppliers and my clients. I've come up with our best solutions by simply taking the time to understand the business model of those we serve and those that serve us in order to serve *our* purpose better.

In other words, I look for a win-win for both sides of the equation when negotiating new business. I try to ensure prompt payment or more favorable terms from new clients through settlement incentives, performance bonuses, profit sharing, or partnering with them on their projects or some other form of contractual arrangement. I also seek a suitable way to reward suppliers for prompt delivery of product or service. This gives me an opportunity to control our financial future and in turn our destiny more tightly. We don't just want to be the supplier of choice to our clients given the terms, but also the client of choice to our *suppliers* given their terms as well. The result, in many instances, was that our businesses got put to the top of the list for both payment and supply, effectively shortening the cash flow gap.

A classic example of this took place with the growth of our property development business. When we launched this company, its core focus was to buy, renovate, and sell residential homes. We started with only $60,000 in working capital—not a lot in the property world, by any stretch of the imagination. But with a little bit of leverage from the bank, we had enough to get one home started. We completed it in record time compared with some of the other stories I was hearing in the market. However, it was still slow relative to our available cash. If we continued working at this rate, we would only ever work on one property at a time. And it was clear that at some point we were going to run out of cash through holding costs if the market slowed for some reason and be forced to sell to the first person who came along with poor eyesight and a full wallet.

So I set about looking at the business's supply chain and attempted to figure out how to shorten the cash flow gap.

On one end, we had real estate agents feeding us property deals on the way in and potential purchasers on the way out. On the other end, we had tradespeople helping with kitchen and bathroom renovations, flooring, painting, and landscaping. Our challenge was to get all of these guys working faster so we could free up some money in our cash flow and get into more deals.

So I pulled the real estate agents aside and offered them a very clear brief on sales and purchases of all deals. I wanted to make it easy to assess deal flow on the way in and speed of sale on the way out. They knew that I made decisions quickly and that they could count on me to not be greedy and to do what I had to so we could get the deal over the line—both on the way in and the way out. Our target was to renovate 12 properties over the next 18 months. Interestingly, while the agents did feed us a lot of deals, they never called back once they sold me the stock. Weird. But we got what we wanted anyway; we had deal flow.

I then took each of our preferred tradespeople aside and offered each one a settlement bonus on delivery. We'd set a completion date for each project, and if they finished the job on time, I would give them 10 percent of the quoted price as a bonus. If they finished later than the completion date, I would take a week longer to pay them for every day they were late.

This did two things for me: It gave me deal flow of potential properties from the agents as I made quick decisions, thereby making their jobs easier. And it got the tradespeople to reno-vate the properties much faster. Some even went back on the market finished in less than three weeks.

In the next 18 months, we did 13 properties. We were on target and on time—and on budget—except for one instance when I got greedy on the sale price. See? The dreaded ego still steps in from time to time.

It took me five companies and a number of years before I was finally honest enough with myself to admit that I could not grow the business in half the time, for half the money, with half the staff. It was only when I *did* get real and invested the time in some financial planning and future forecasting that we actually started to make some money in the various professional investments we had.

When I look back, all of my mistakes boiled down to ego. When I forecast an aggressive and optimistic plan, my ego got in the way of reality. When I was conservative and honest, my forecast was based on my ability.

My next money lessons went hand in hand with everything I'd learned about time efficiency and strategy. So, to avoid constant financial panic in our businesses, I set about schedul-ing "money meetings." These were moments during each day, week, month, quarter, and year that I would consciously stop and focus on where the money was coming from, where it was going, and how fast it was doing both. And these were not meetings to just go over profit and loss statements or to assess sales reports for the week. These were opportunities for us to take a closer look at where we were headed financially in the future. I kept the planning sessions in line with my philosophy and spent time during each to focus on how I could *first* plan better for *what* was coming in the future, and *then* work out *how* I was going to cover that before I needed to.

The simple reason that companies find themselves in financial strife is that they are typically unprepared—or at least, underprepared.

Just look at how many businesses get into a total spin come the end of the financial year. We all know it's coming, because it does every year at the same time. That's why it's called the end of the financial year ... because it's at the end. The last day. It's over. Done. Finished. And yet, we react with total surprise, as if someone has reshuffled the date cards of life. We act as if we had no idea the end was coming and then set about creating total panic in the workplace when it arrives.

But don't feel bad. It's such a common small business habit to leave all of our financial planning until the last minute. After all, that's not your job as a company leader. I mean, that responsibility belongs to your bookkeeper or accountants—right? Yeah right!

We spend all year running around, worrying about making money but then spend almost no time managing the money we've made.

And then we wonder why we don't have as much money as we thought we had; some of it just seemed to, well, disappear. Where did it go, we wonder? We're sure it was there yesterday. We know we *made* the money—so why isn't it in the bank today?

Of course, a lot of these questions can be answered with stronger financial controls, processes, and cash flow management. But many of them can also be addressed with basic, easy, simple, forward planning. I learned that the first thing this required was my commitment to first determine what I needed to achieve financially in my businesses and then how I was going to pay for it.

During our daily morning updates my accounts person would report on the money that came in yesterday, on what she was chasing today, and what had to be paid tomorrow. At our weekly Monday administration meetings the focus was on cash flow management and forecasting the next 30 days of potential income and expenses. To assist us in these meetings, the sales team would prep us with a report on expected income, the production team on expected expenses. And the accounts team would match the two.

We'd then set aside time at our quarterly business planning strategy summits to update our tax plan through the end of the financial year to make sure we were on track with what was ahead of us. This was also our time to forecast and identify first what we needed to purchase in the way of big-ticket items in the next quarter and then how to establish the cash flow to accommodate that.

We'd also meet twice yearly for a two-day company strategy retreat. Our financial planning at these meetings was focused on our reality check for the next half year. This is when we'd all review and be honest about our targets and admit whether we thought we were going to make them. This was our most important financial metric for the year. Too many business leaders rule by fear when it comes to forecasting sales in their businesses. They stand in front of their sales teams and *tell* them what they need to sell for the year without asking the teams if they feel they can actually sell that much. The net result is that the owner gets frustrated when targets are not met, and the sales teams get deflated when they continually get a bollocking from the owner or sales manager. It's very counterproductive to the cause.

I found that the key here was to say to the team, "Tell me honestly, what do you *really* think you can sell in the next half year? Will you hit the targets we set, or do we need to revise them?" I'd then ask everyone the question, "*How* are we going to adjust the financial plan to suit that sales forecast and still deliver our desired profit?"

Putting these simple financial metrics in place made us far more accurate and honest about our financial future. We were going about our business without panic, since we knew exactly what was ahead of us and how we were going to deal with it.

Real Money!

Three things you need to do now to Future-Proof Your Business and make sure you are working with real money.

Action One

What is the truth about the financial situation in your business? Do you continually rob Peter to pay Paul? If you do—*stop it!*

Action Two

If you had to run your business on vapor, what would you cut out? Why have you not done that already? Sit down each month and go over the numbers. Strive to be *always* lean and mean and never fat and lazy in the business—no matter what the economic climate.

Action Three

Get some financial rhythm in the business, weekly metrics, monthly performance indicators, and annual planning events. Good financial planning is not just about forecasting; it's about understanding the things that will influence your business in the future and *matching* that against your forecast.

Meaningful Marketing

"We looked successful in the eyes of our potential customers, and, as a result, everything that came out of my mouth had an air of credibility to it. Perception is reality."

Now that you're armed with an understanding of your company's *internal* positioning, it's time to step out into the real world.

When we opened our recording studio in the early 1990s, business was not going so well. We'd had the doors open for just over 12 months—and it was tough. We thought we were doing all the right things, but the market was just not responding—and it was largely our own fault. We'd positioned ourselves as great advertising jingle writers and producers, but operating in the middle of a recession with shrinking advertising budgets meant that our service was one of the first things to get cut. Advertising agencies, our core source of revenue, were hell-bent on making their clients' dollars go a little further. Many of them perceived our product and service offers to be a luxury item—something that they could do without if they needed to save a buck on the overall advertisement production.

We were mailing out material and making calls to any and every potential client we could think of, but we were just not getting the message across. I'd run out of ideas about how to get us back on the radar and show our clients that we were an important part of the creative mix—and that they really *did* need us to get the best results. One afternoon I found myself at the house of one of my early business mentors, Graham Hogg. I was having a beer with his son and my best mate, Peter. Graham came in after work and sat next to us at the bar.

"So, where have you been today?" he asked me inquisitively. I answered (somewhat defensively), "At work, of course."

He gave me the once-over and grinned. "Hmph ... at work, huh? You look like you've been at the beach—faded jeans, sneakers, t-shirt—is that what you wear to work?" he continued to probe.

"Sure, I'm in the recording business. It's rock and roll, it's hip," I laughed back.

But he kept digging. "So, how's business going?"

I paused for a moment as thoughts flashed through my head and searched for the right thing to say with the most positive possible spin, but I had nothin'. I lifted my spirits as best I could to deliver the answer with honesty, laced with an air of optimism. "Not so great, actually. We just can't seem to get anyone to spend money in this economic climate, but I am sure it'll come around." Despite my quiet, confident bravado, my tired voice revealed my despair.

Graham pressed on. "So how much do you charge for your services?"

By now, I could sense that this might be going somewhere. I also began to think that there might be a slap coming. "About $5,000 a jingle," I replied.

There was a pause before the next question. "So, do you reckon you look like a bloke that I would trust $5,000 of my hard-earned money with?"

I looked at him and had to ask the question, even though I guessed I knew the answer. "I'm not sure what you mean. I don't look trustworthy?"

"You've missed the point," he barked back. "You don't look like you *want* my money or that you would do a good job with it if I gave it to you. You look more like you want to be a roadie in a rock band. *Get dressed!* Show me you mean business and you are professional. Perception *is* reality, and right now my perception of you is that you're an amateur, a newbie, a new kid on the block who does not know what he's doing and who probably won't even be in business come Monday."

And with that, he left us at the bar.

The next day, I got up and got dressed for work. Just as I was about to walk out the door, I did a double-take in the mirror. Graham was right. I *didn't* look like I was in business; I looked like someone who was playing with sounds in my studio all day. So later that day, I went out and bought myself a decent suit, tie, shirt, cufflinks, shoes, a proper briefcase, and I sat down and created some stronger presentation tools for my meetings. Then I scraped together all the extra money I had and bought myself an older, but very presentable, Range Rover.

And wouldn't you know it . . . it *worked.* All of a sudden, we looked like we meant business. Because we looked like the successful business we wanted to be in the future in the eyes of our potential customers, everything that came out of my mouth had an air of credibility to it. It appeared to them that I really did know what I was talking about, and business started to lift.

That was my first lesson in marketing.

I realized that before I bothered to send any message to the market, my business promise and positioning needed to match that message.

Our message had previously said: We're professional and good at what we do. But our look was saying: We're sloppy and we really don't care. Once I had corrected our perception and positioning, I could develop a strategy to market the business. Then we could cover the tactical matters—like *how* we were going to get our message to our potential audience.

You see, one of the most common fatal mistakes that businesspeople make is focusing on the tactical elements of marketing *before* they get the marketing platform in shape. They anguish over what flyer to create, what letter to send, what color it should be, what font the type should be in, and where they should advertise their business—when they should instead begin the entire process by taking a strategic look at how they want to market their business.

And that is one of the killers in developing a marketing strategy: So many business leaders start by concentrating on their advertising message of today rather than their marketing positioning of the future. They do this because they assume that advertising and marketing are one and the same. They are often used in the same sentence to describe a process assisting a sale, and they work hand in hand to develop solid strategies. However, they have very different roles in an overall plan.

In basic terms, *advertising* encompasses the mass market and covers the elements of communication where you display your product or service to a number of potential customers at the same time through various media like television, radio, press, and magazines. *Marketing* is the strategy that you use to communicate with your customers—be it direct mail, building relationships, loyalty programs, unique packaging, or advertising. In fact, it covers any means of interaction that involves making contact with your customers to offer your products or services to them.

In order for you to effectively utilize a strong advertising strategy today, you first must have a solid marketing plan in place to ensure your market positioning of the future.

While this may sound a little confusing, the easiest way to begin is to understand how you can combine the two elements and then make them work together through an integrated strategy.

So what is marketing all about?

Well, here's what I've come to believe, and here's how we've tried to simplify the marketing strategy in over 20 years of consulting. We've used this method with some of the biggest brands across the planet; it's simple, it's robust, and it's easy for everyone to understand.

Now, before I get started, let me say that some marketing experts will read the next few pages and proclaim that "It's just not that simple; there are much deeper issues to consider, more focus groups to be had, more reports to be written, more understanding of your value proposition, more consumer impact studies to be conducted, more market research to be developed, and much more thought put into it if you are to be successful."

And I agree, in part. Sure, we could all sit around, and invest a heap of time and money contemplating our navels. We might even gather some helpful information this way. But most people in small business simply don't have the money or resources to invest in their businesses to achieve that. It would be nice for sure, but in many cases just not practical. But as we've already established, we can take some *time* to create good strategy.

We can create solid marketing strategy for our businesses if we just take time to stop and think about how we want to position that business in the future. And we can start the process by asking ourselves some really straightforward questions today:

- Who is our target customer?
- What is it we are trying to sell them and what purpose does it serve them?
- Why would they care?

- What is the market opportunity for the business, what would customers pay, how many of them would pay, and why would they pay us and not one of our competitors?

The questions seem simple and even somewhat common-sense. And for sure if you are in business you would have an intuitive answer to all of them. But before we move on to create a solid positioning and strategy for your business, take a look back over the answers to the questions and double-check yourself that you are still on track with those answers.

Everywhere you look, companies are jostling for a competitive edge—that unique difference that makes their product or service better than someone else's. They're offering buy-one-get-one-free; lifetime warranties; six months interest-free; free deliveries; money-back guarantees; cheaper, faster, everywhere, louder, or brighter. It is relentless, and for most companies, finding that edge is a nightmare.

Every day, your customers are faced with literally *thousands* of advertising and marketing messages. You can't escape them; they're indoor, outdoor, on the box, in the box, printed, and painted. They irritate, exaggerate, and sometimes even motivate. But most of all, they communicate. Like it or not, people (like you) react to advertising and marketing messages. If they didn't, a lot of people would be out of work—or out of business. And since the average consumer will only remember a small percentage of the messages he sees or hears, it's no wonder that so many business leaders can't see the value in their advertising and marketing expenditure.

A lot of this has to do with the way their businesses are positioned in the minds of their consumers. They are not clear on what they stand for or what they mean to the consumer and often try to be all things to all people.

Because of the volume of information in the marketplace, people who are looking to promote their businesses have a series of hurdles to overcome in order for their message to be heard.

In an effort to break through the clutter, one of the biggest traps that many fall into is to opt for a quick-fix advertising campaign—something that's more or less a cash flow Band-Aid. This is what happens when companies are *reactive* rather than *proactive*. The blinkers go on, and they worry about the short-term effect on the bank balance rather than the business's future marketplace positioning.

They stumble from one reactive campaign to another, from one bright idea to the next, disaster to disaster as the opposition heads them off at every pass. By the time they have come out of one battle, they find themselves in the middle of another as another competitor has moved in for an attack.

The result is that they do what so many businesspeople should not do: They panic and drop their prices. They take this approach in favor of developing strong, specific, and deliberate long-term positioning of their business in the marketplace—a positioning that would give them the stability of a future they continually seek, but do not take the time to strategically create.

A by-product of this trend is the lack of vital transactional drivers in the business like service, quality, relationship, and ease. Remember—these elements offer the perception of value, and if present in all forms, can in many instances remove the need for discounting.

But once you've gone the discounting route, it's all downhill! A price war will inevitably follow as competitors slug it out, believing this is the only way to win. In reality, the only thing that is inevitable about a price war is that at least one of the companies will die as margins are squeezed. And there's no guarantee that it won't be *yours*. Unless you are a seasoned professional discounter, with a business that has a model based on discount sales and providing products and services to fulfill that price point and trade efficiently on that reduced margin, then only one thing can be sure in a discount war: You lose control of your future as the market dictates it for you.

In order to market successfully, each individual campaign
has to become part of an overall market positioning strategy.

Most importantly, be honest with yourself when evaluating
the impact of both your campaigns and your competitors on
your business. By taking a long-term view on your positioning,
you can move to a second campaign while the opposition is
still focusing on the first one. A long-term strategic approach
also allows your company some breathing space, or a head
start, so you can concentrate on winning through staged,
tactical campaigns over an extended period of time.

Part of this positioning requires that your customers will
care about what you are saying to them. It is easy for companies
to get too close to your product. After all, you're the best at
what you do, aren't you? But do your customers see it that way?
Do they really care about what you have to say to them? Are
you looking from the outside in when considering the way you
market your business, or are you taking a very limited view of
the situation and completely missing the point?

Put simply: Do your customers have the same view of you
as you do? Or do you just assume they do?

I mentioned previously that between my speaking engagements and business commitments, I spend over half the year
in hotels. For years, I have been fortunate enough to stay at
some of the best hotels in the world—marble staircases, grand
entrances, people opening doors for you, rooms so big you could
play football in them. Fantastic, isn't it? Not for me.

I have simple expectations for an ideal hotel. I want a quick
check-in, a steam iron in the room so I can make my shirts flat
and I don't look like I've been sleeping in them, and a remote
control for the TV I can understand. But do they know that?
I figure that if I am spending that much time in their hotels,
then someone, somewhere might like to give me a call or send
a letter sometime to find out what makes me tick. You'd think

that this might just help them with the positioning of their offer to me as a consumer, right?

I live with disappointment, though, because this has only happened to me twice: once at a hotel in Darwin in the Northern Territory of Australia and once in Kuala Lumpur, Malaysia. While the rest have simply made assumptions, these are the only hotels to have ever bothered to ask about my preferences. And because they have asked, they're also aware that while I may only stay at their hotels for a few nights at a time, I *do* have some influence over a much larger audience—and because of this, I am able to help them with their marketing cause. After all, my role as a professional speaker means that I'm often asked about potential venues to hold conferences.

But I continue to go through the interrogation of repeating my name, address, and phone number when I check in to the same venues. I still have to wait for a steam iron to come from housekeeping, and I still get frustrated as I press the wrong buttons on the remote. If someone could just guarantee those three simple requests would be met, they would have my business for life. And believe it or not, it's that easy in your business, too. You just need to *ask* what your customers want—and then position your message around the answer.

It's also critical that when you're figuring out what to say to your customers, that you're clear on how you gather the information to help you say it. Look for hot buttons that turn your customers on to your product or service and not *assume* that you know what they think.

Remember, as far as your customers are concerned, how they *perceive* your product or service is the way it is. If you can get a clearer picture on how you're positioned in the marketplace, you have an excellent platform upon which to build your communication with the market and get your message right.

You see, your customers are pretty simple people, really, and we marketers occasionally overcomplicate our strategies by attempting to make them too clever. And while these witty marketing messages might win awards, they won't necessarily sell more products; sometimes, they are just too slick. That's why we like to bring it right back to basics. Make it easy for customers to understand, so they can see just how easy it is to do business with you.

We've come to realize over the years that in order to significantly impact our customers, we need to integrate all of our marketing messages over a number of levels, and we've broken our marketing strategy into the six following key components to help us do just that.

1. **Brand Marketing.** Activities performed to increase the awareness and value of our brand.
2. **Area Marketing.** This can be done in two ways:
   a. Promote the business in a regional area, state, or territory.
   b. Promote a specific area, such as a single product or service that we're offering.
3. **Relationship Marketing.** A strategy designed to build better relationships and increase customer loyalty and repeat business.
4. **Local Area Marketing.** The aim of this approach is to become an active member of the local community, a good corporate citizen, and leverage local relationships.
5. **Information Technology.** This part of the strategy incorporates anything we do online: e-mail marketing, e-commerce, search engine optimization, social media, and so forth.
6. **Training.** It's all well and good to build a marketing strategy, but if nobody knows what that means to them, then all is lost. Without companywide marketing training, the frontline troops will have no idea what they are supposed to be selling when the customers come in.

Let me give you a little more detail on the focus for each area in our strategy.

The Brand Marketing Strategy

The brand element of your marketing strategy should be all about building brand value in your business. How are you going to make what you do unique so that when I think of a product in your category, I relate that *directly* to your brand? Some excellent examples of this are Hoover, Kleenex, Xerox, Aspirin. These are all examples of brands where the brand has *become* the category in most people's everyday lives. Someone might say "Hoover that up for me, please," instead of, "Can you vacuum that?" Or, "Hand me a Kleenex," instead of a tissue. In the 1970s the boss might have requested that you "Xerox that for me," instead of photocopying that. And many people will ask for "an aspirin," not "some Ibuprofen."

I learned this lesson very early on, during my recording studio business adventure. Of course, a new business has no brand value at all, and building that value is a very slow process, particularly when you have a limited budget.

Most businesses embrace advertising activity to build their brands and brand value. However, if you rely on just your advertising to do that for you, then you're going to end up spending a lot of money to get your return. Can you afford to do that?

My first company had no money to do anything, let alone advertise. In fact, every time we made a sale, I'd print out a bank statement just so that I could stare lovingly at the balance. In order to get our message into the streets and make some noise, we used public relations activity and guerrilla marketing tactics as our cornerstones for building brand value. We'd do crazy stunts to attract media attention and be prolific about commenting on issues to the media when something came up in our business category.

One day, while sitting around the office of our recording studio (telepathically willing the phone to ring), we came up with the idea of using the spare time in the studio to record some things we might be able to sell as prepackaged jingles. Not a bad idea, but we still needed to get our brand known in the marketplace as a business that could actually do the job and do it well. And we had to do it in a crappy economic climate when nobody was really listening to us and nobody really seemed to care.

So, rather than using our copious amount of spare time to write a book on "94 ways to eat baked beans," we decided to write a song about the crappy economic climate. We wrote and recorded a comedy rap song called "The Recession Rap" about the politicians and bankers of the day—the major media characters surrounding the recession. We got some puppeteers to play the characters and do the film clip with us, and then sent it off to a number of record publishers. Much to our delight, well-known music company EMI loved the idea and decided to release it for us—and *bang*! All of a sudden, we found ourselves with a Top 40 hit on the charts with the song nominated for an ARIA award (the Australian version of the Grammys).

This gave us great media coverage, a reason to talk to clients, and some credibility in the marketplace as "the guys who did that song." And away we went. Finally, after months of getting our mates to call the office phone just to make sure it was still working and day in, day out, wondering if we were ever going to survive in business, the phone started to ring, with real clients calling! And to this day, 20 years down the road, I use this style of marketing as a means of building my business brand: me.

I write for a number of magazines and newspapers on a regular basis. I've hosted two national network business television shows. I regularly comment on business issues in the press and on radio. And I pitch anything I do as much as I can to the media if I think they might be able to pull a story out of it. Yes, it can be time-consuming for me, but the brand value we get from the media for this activity is far more than I could afford to get if I paid for the advertising space. In some instances, I even get paid to conduct some of this activity. So my marketing strategy essentially funds itself.

My challenge for you is this: Figure out what you can do to get the media interested in your business. And I'm not talking about telling them it's your business's first birthday celebration—yawn. Where's the excitement in *that*? I'm talking about a meaningful message you can use to have them build your brand with you. Do you have some great invention for your industry? Are you doing business in your category in an incredibly stand-out, drop-dead, cutting-edge innovative fashion? Did you make a cutting, controversial comment to the media that might get you noticed? What is unique about you or your business?

Nowadays, I'm the bloke on the television and radio declaring that if businesses are to get through tough economic times, they need to stop blaming the government or the financial institutions or the banks and get on with it. It may well be a tough message for them to hear from a bloke they might hire to work for them. But, it gets a run—and our phone is still ringing.

Although some of these crazy, unusual, or left-field guerrilla tactics might be good for your business, make sure the activity you do today still matches the positioning you want for the future. That our recording business had a Top 40 hit, and a creative one at that, gave us the perfect positioning as the guys who do a quality job with creative flair.

The Area Marketing Strategy

Very early on in my business career, I learned that in order to get my message to my customer, I needed to create a simple, clear, and concise message. I learned that we needed to adopt a simple theory with our marketing messages, "*less* is more." Less content, more focus, less words, more specific message in the words we did use. Makes sense, really; people just don't take notice of clutter or noise in their day, so why would we clutter them up with our marketing messages and expect they will understand what it is we are trying to say to them?

And yet, we do clutter their day, day in, day out, as we try and get every message we want to say to them delivered to them in the short space of time we have to say it.

Stop it.

Seek to break the marketing messages you deliver to your customers into *areas* of focus in your business. These areas might be geographic, demographic, or simply different products or services you might have to offer. Whatever they may be, look to focus on *one* area with each message. This gives your customers the best opportunity to understand what it is you have to offer them. The simplicity is to consider what message *you* remember in a day. Use that as your yardstick for your customers.

Our consulting business worked for a hotel chain in Australia for a number of years; our brief was to help them with the marketing message. I can recall a classic conversation with one of the hotel managers one day. He called, most disturbed that his marketing campaign for a Valentine's Day dinner promotion was "not working nearly as well as it should be." I calmed him down on the phone and said simply, "Send me the advertisements you've been running." On receipt of the campaign materials, it was clear his problem was that he was simply unclear to his customers.

I rang him back and said, "Mate, you've got a paper advertisement here that talks about the special Valentine's Day dinner you have on, the sports bar specials you are running, the pool competition you have on Wednesday nights, the specials in the liquor store, and the fact that you offer senior discounts. . . . Who the hell are you talking to in this message? His response: "Well, all of our customers." I said, "So are all of these customers people who would come to your Valentine's dinner?" Sheepishly he responded, "Mate, if you could see some of the blokes who come to the pool night or the sports bar, you'd wonder if they could eat with cutlery, let alone take a date to dinner." . . . And there lies my point.

Seek to target those customers who you feel will be the most likely to respond to your simple, focused message and the area of your business you wish to promote. Fill the Valentine's Day dinner and then talk about how you are going to promote sports night or the pool competition.

One message, one area of the business to target, targeted to one target audience.

The Relationship Marketing Strategy

It took me awhile to determine exactly where in my company the real sales development was coming from. For years, I just assumed that more clients equals more sales equals more money equals bigger business. So that was our mantra: More equals more.

Until I figured out that all I needed to do was to apply the same rule I did with our area campaign where *less* is actually more.

When you think about it, there are only three *real* ways that your company can increase sales:

1. Sell more to your existing customers.
2. Sell the same amount of the same product or service to the same existing customers at a higher price.
3. Find more customers.

Ponder that for a moment, because there are so many people in business who seem to forget that simple but true fact.

Of these three sales development opportunities, the first one is the easiest by far. After all, you are already spending time talking to your current customers; they already know you and love you. So why not keep talking to them more often until you know you have all their business, and they simply cannot purchase any more from you?

Why is it that companies seem to be perpetually chasing the *next* customer or the *next* deal when these customers don't know them—or, for that matter, care about them? Why spend good time and money chasing what's next when they haven't fully developed the customers they have to their full potential?

Why look for new business when they have not nearly exhausted the opportunities they already have with existing customers?

However, to do this, you're going to need to build strong customer relationships.

Now, let me clarify the term "customer relationship." This is not just about you being a good bloke and providing good service when potential purchasers come into your business or call you to buy something. They're just doing what they have to do to get on with their day and fulfill a need that they have, and you're just doing your job. Quality customer relationships come when *you* seek *them* out, when *you* make the effort to build those connections into something meaningful. And in many cases, this takes place outside of the contact you have with them during normal business transactions.

Consider this question for a moment: Who was the person who sold you your last house, car, washing machine, couch, dishwasher, or TV? These are all significant purchases. Yet the people from whom you bought them have likely faded into oblivion by now, mainly due to the fact that they failed to maintain a relationship with you after the purchase. Therefore, you moved on, and eventually forgot about them. Many of these salespeople were also too busy looking for the next customer instead of attempting to secure further purchases from you—possibly for the rest of your life.

It's crazy, really, when you do the math:

- A lifetime of houses has to be good for at least two or three sales.
- A lot of people turn over their cars every three to five years.
- You might be lucky to get 10 years out of your washing machine before another one will be necessary.

- Your couch is probably only good for about three to five years before the springs go or the material fades.
- At the rate you put dishes through the washer, you'd reckon there's only five to seven years in that one as well.
- And televisions nowadays are changing so fast that you're bound to want a new one inside of five years.

This is a lesson I learned very clearly during the years that I was trading in residential property. We sold 13 renovated properties in 18 months, and do you know how many real estate salespeople called me back after they sold me a property? *None*. Not one. Yet, if just one salesperson had bothered to follow me in and out of each deal, that person would have made a decent year's salary in commissions from working with a single client: me.

On settlement day, when the home was ours I'd say, "Give me a call in a month, and we'll put it back on the market." You can't get much more direct than that! I had proved to them that I was an easy client; I was honest and made decisions quickly. But once they had the sale on the way in to the property, they forgot about me on the way out. It's just another classic example of someone looking for their next client when the next client is right there under their nose.

Fast-forward 10 years.

I was admittedly operating in the same way that the realtors had been.

I was so focused on chasing more clients—*any* clients—that I had forgotten where the money was really coming from: our existing clients.

These were the people who had stuck by us over the years and continued to see the value in what we did. I'd forgotten my own experience with the real estate agents, and I became the one who was so focused on "next" that I forgot to look after the "now." It was time for my company to get back to basics and remember some of the relationship skills we already knew.

And it wasn't that hard. Here are a few of the simple things we did to build better relationships:

- I made a point of calling each and every one of our clients personally at least every three months just to say G'day and ask how they were doing—and if we were doing what we were supposed to be doing.

- We went back to sending flowers or small gifts after every project to thank customers for their business.

- We scheduled weekly "little lunches" with one client at a time. These weren't the long boozy client lunches we all knew from the 1980s that went all afternoon; these were simply one of our guys turning up at the client's office at about 10:30 A.M. with muffins, cake, and coffee, just to share a snack and a chat with them. A little lunch with a big impact, and all done in an hour.

- We remembered to send out birthday cards and gifts. Simple, but effective.

- We restarted our monthly newsletter—but not to brag about the things we were doing. Rather, we created a short note or paragraph on something that would interest our clients about their businesses. And we crafted it to each person's preferences to make them feel as though it was their very own personalized message.

- We developed an online project tracking system that allowed clients to dial in at any time and see where the project was in the production process.

- And we changed the way we looked at business development and started to focus more internally on "client development" at our sales meetings. We talked about how we could grow clients' businesses and have them spend more money with us throughout the year, as opposed to always seeking new clients.

As part of our relationship marketing strategy development, we also put a few communication rules in place in the business.

We realized that we had to learn how to talk *to* our customers in a more meaningful fashion if we were to sell them more products and services.

By simply conducting some client surveys, we discovered that we were delivering our communication to them in a language *we* wanted to use as opposed to one they would like to hear. In short, we were being lazy; we were talking *at* them instead of *to* them. We also needed to work on what messages we were sending them, so that they received a clear promise from us in those messages. And we needed to deliver those messages with passion.

Once we had our heads around that, we began to ensure that all of the information we were sending them was about them—not us. I looked back over some of our communication about how "good" we were, and I realized that we sounded like a bunch of egotistical jocks. *I* didn't even like me when I read that material. Once we removed the ego from the messages, they suddenly seemed genuine—like we actually meant what we said instead of spouting a bunch of rhetorical crap on a page in a newsletter or in a paragraph in an e-mail.

In summary, we needed to be more aware of what we said, how we said it, why we said it, and when we said it.

Our next step was to turn relationship marketing into a companywide habit, which meant that we had to develop a tactical calendar of events to guarantee that we employed a consistent strategy with our clients. But in order to have a range of different things to discuss with our clients, we needed information about them other than simply what they bought from us. How did we find this out? Well, we talked to them.

It's amazing what you can find out from somebody just by asking questions.

A few years ago, I was out shopping for a new car. I had a great sales guy who I had been dealing with for a number of years at Mercedes Benz. I called him and said, "I need a new car, and I want it to be able to change gears. I don't want an automatic." To his credit, he responded with, "I can't sell you one like that. If I did, you'd hate me, because you'd never be able to get rid of it. They just don't sell very well in Mercedes Benz models."

Instead, this dealer found me another bloke to help me out. Upon arriving at his dealership, we hit the road for a lengthy test drive. Along the way, my new sales mate started to ask me more questions, as if in passing. "So Troy, what do you do on weekends? Do you play a sport? Are you married? Do you have any kids? What hobbies do you like? Who is your favorite football team?" In just over 45 minutes, this bloke practically extracted my life story. And I thought he was just a nice guy having a chat.

By the time we got back from our drive, it was just a matter of him steering me to the right car. I ended up buying one from him, and I figured that would be the last I'd hear from him. I assumed, as with most car sales guys, that he simply wouldn't bother to talk to me again. He'd be off working on his next deal.

Not this bloke.

After he made the sale, I heard from him about every four to six weeks.

"Hey Troy, I've got a few tickets to the football on Saturday night. Since your team is playing, I'll drop them off to you."

"Hey Troy, I've got some information on some new ceramic brakes you might be interested in for the racecar. I'll send it off to your race mechanic if you can give me his name."

"Hey Troy, I've just put an information pack into the post to you for a driving tour in Germany you were telling me you were interested in. If you have any questions, give me a call and I can hook you up with the tour guide."

Over the course of two years, he'd take the opportunity to reach out to help me with something I was interested in. He made it all about me and all about building our relationship. Not once did he try to sell me another car. Until ... "Hey Troy—you said you'd be interested in another car in about two years. Well, it's been just about two years; so do you want to talk about that?" What do you reckon I'm going to say, "Of course! Sure, mate, I'll drop in for a chat sometime soon."

I was ready to buy because of the relationship he'd built with me over that time. And not only has he got my business, he has sold almost $1.5 million worth of cars to my mates on my recommendation. That certainly can't be a bad thing.

Do that math: My mates and I turning over $1 million plus in cars every two or three years equals some pretty good commissions! And all of it came because of the connection he spent time making with a single existing client. Then consider how many other blokes my mates have referred to him over the last few years as a result of their dealings with him. Multiply that number and see it add up—wow!

The Local Marketing Strategy

As the market shrinks and media options increase on a yearly basis, the micro marketing picture becomes a far more important element for your business. It's even more critical nowadays to focus on your own backyard—your micro market. I've found for the many brands I've been a consultant for and the various companies I've owned that local marketing strategy is often the key to success. It provides the best opportunity to leverage the brand exposure in the marketplace with little expenditure.

But—and there is a big but—in order for local marketing to be effective, you must commit to the program's success. And that means you need to commit the time to make the program a success. That's the only way it's going to work.

So where do you start?

The simple goals of any local marketing campaign are to build brand awareness, and develop a reputation as a good corporate citizen. Local marketing is all about getting involved with community groups, businesses, sporting teams, or charitable organizations—really, any segment of people in your neighborhood or area who might benefit from an association with your business.

The first step in your plan is to produce a list of the following:

- **Sporting clubs in the area**. Start by finding out which clubs or teams your staff members are involved in. Gather details such as contact names, offices held, and phone numbers.

- **Addresses and phone numbers of businesses in your local area** that may use your services for one reason or another.

- **Charity events in your area.** Contact the community newspaper or local government and ask if they know of any upcoming events.

- **Community groups in your area.** Gather contact information and meeting addresses for groups such as Scouts, Guides, Toastmasters, and so on.

- **Government or quasi-governmental offices in your area,** related officers or staff members, and their address and phone numbers.

- **Contact details of the local newspaper in your area,** ensuring that you track down information for both local and metro publications.

- **All schools, both state and private**. You can sometimes get this list from the Department of Education. From time to time, there will be activities in which your company can become involved or programs you might be able to sponsor.

All of these lists are vital to planning and analyzing your local marketing strategy. It is important to spend some time compiling the correct information, as many of the programs in your plan will revolve around these contacts. You can find most of the information you need in the telephone book, local directories, online sources, or even by ringing your local council or community newspaper.

To place your local marketing activities week into perspective with other daily and weekly duties, you'll need to put this information into a calendar. A calendar will allow you to realistically assess what you can achieve in any given week. Allow for three to four hours a week initially, then try to consolidate this to about one to two hours a week. This should be enough to give your campaign some momentum without taking your focus away from day-to-day business.

Now that you've got that done, what are you supposed to do next? That's a question I receive from professionals all over the world. "Okay, so I've done it. You've made me compile these lists of different things—what are they all supposed to mean to me? Where do I start?"

Well, the best place to start is to conduct what I call an "opportunity audit." This involves matching some of the people and places you've written on your list to the opportunities you might be able to create to work or partner with them on projects that might introduce you to new groups of potential clients or customers.

Here's an example of how the opportunity audit works.

We owned our pizza shop during a particularly tough market. Because we were trying to turn the business around, we were working like mad in the local markets surrounding the store. We gathered all of the staff as well as some outsiders who we brought in as extra creative minds, and we spent the afternoon brainstorming ideas on how to leverage ourselves in the marketplace and develop our opportunity audit. The outcome was a great local marketing calendar for the next six months, designed to give us the best opportunity for brand development and community loyalty.

There were several local marketing campaign components to the plan. First, we sent free pizza to all of the hairdressers in the neighborhood each weekend for lunch. We knew full well that they would spend the afternoon telling their clients "what wonderful boys we were for feeding them every weekend." We sent letters to all of the area real estate agents' clients welcoming people to their new neighborhoods by sending free pizza on their first night in their new home.

We sent free pizza to the local university recreation club on a Friday night, knowing that students are pretty brand loyal when they get something for nothing. We also made deals with the area sports clubs and charity groups, and gave tours to local schools, showing them how pizza is made and treating them to lunch after the tour of the store.

They were all simple, easy-to-execute tactics designed to get us further entrenched in the local community. And they worked!

The Internet Marketing Strategy

In the late 1990s, marketing strategies across the world shifted from "high touch" to "high tech." We stopped calling people and started e-mailing them. We stopped sending personalized letters and started texting shorter messages. We stopped conducting sales calls and started sending people to our web sites. We stopped answering the phone when someone called in to our offices and instead let our electronic voice tell them to "press 1" to talk to someone. Or in some cases press 15 buttons to get bounced around the world through six different call centers only to get cut off 30 minutes later.

I've got this neat party trick I do on stage when I am speaking. I pull out my BlackBerry halfway through my presentation just to see who's called me in the last half hour. While I usually get a mix of 20-plus e-mails and three or four text messages, it's rare that I have a missed call—proof that we're still cutting corners when it comes to building relationships through technology and favoring the route where we don't have to talk to anyone.

Sure, text, e-mail, web sites, blogs, online forums, e-commerce, and m-commerce are all good marketing ideas; but they do take the soul out of the sales pitch to some degree.

This trend became even more apparent to me upon purchasing a technology company in 2001. When my partners and I moved into the business, we were horrified to see the extreme emphasis that was placed on marketing via technology. The philosophy was that as a technology company, we should show our clients our expertise by using it to communicate with them.

What a total crock. It was nothing more than an excuse for a bunch of lazy sales guys and technology geeks to not talk to their clients. And trust me—that was a good thing for some of them; they struggled to even have a conversation with other staff members. It was as if previous management only let them out of their offices for an hour or so a week and just slid pizza and Mountain Dew under the door of their offices the rest of the time.

Our first challenge was to turn this "no touch" culture around and find a way to use technology and get the soul back into our sales pitch. We started by having our sales team call each and every one of the 2,500 current clients in our database. These were people who had not been spoken to by a human being from our office in *years*! We then had them call the 2,000 potential clients in the database. Only then did we put clients into a monthly e-mail marketing program—and we only ever sent them information that was relevant to their needs and the daily issues they needed to solve.

The outcome: We put the business back in the black just by calling clients and not sending out nameless, irrelevant pro forma e-mails to them once a quarter.

Over the years, many of us have learned the error of our lazy ways, communicating behind the cover of technology. We're now coming back to shaking hands and kissing babies to get our messages out there. We're figuring out how to develop a combination of high-tech and high-touch in our marketing. In fact, this balance should be central to your Internet marketing strategy. So embrace technology in your marketing, but don't let it control the flow of information, communication, and contact with your customers.

The Marketing Training Strategy

This is the home stretch of the marketing strategy. It's one thing to build a great marketing strategy; it's something else entirely to implement it. And you can only do this if you have the support of your team.

I remember hearing about an interview with the late Charlie Bell, former CEO of McDonald's in Australia (and later McDonald's worldwide). The journalist said to him, "You spend a considerable amount of money on marketing the brand here. How many people do you have in your marketing department in Australia?" His answer was simple, direct, and matter of fact: "We have 15,000. Every person in a uniform is in the marketing department at McDonald's." It was a comment that resonated with me at the time as being one of the most profound things I had heard a marketer say.

And it makes perfect sense when you think about it: You spend considerable amounts of time and money on your marketing efforts. If your frontline employees have no idea about the marketing campaign, the advertising you are running, the promotion you're offering, or how to sell the product or service you've been marketing, then you're essentially wasting your efforts.

Charlie Bell's comment helped me understand that we needed to ensure that each and every marketing strategy we developed for *any* business had a strong training element. Every employee needed to know exactly what was going on and what his role was in marketing the company. In fact, one of the simple, key strategies we've developed has been to make marketing a highlight topic in every staff meeting and to put it first on the agenda so that it's always top of mind.

We accompany every marketing strategy we develop with a training meeting and corresponding documents. We cover each element of the campaign, roles and responsibilities, and the outcomes we're seeking from everyone in the business. It does not need to be complicated—just clear. This also gives us a chance to road test the strategy before we roll it out as we're getting feedback from the team members who actually have to implement that strategy in the field.

By putting all six elements of the marketing strategy into action at the same time, you end up with a solid, integrated approach to your marketing and clarity of positioning for your brand of the future.

The result is that your current and targeted potential clients receive a more consistent message from you more often, which makes it easier for you to distribute information about your brand efficiently and effectively throughout the market to help you secure that client of the future.

Real Marketing Messages!

Three things you need to do now to Future-Proof Your Business and make sure you're creating truly meaningful marketing messages.

Action One

How many levels do you have in your marketing campaign? What are you going to do to build this campaign out into all levels?

(continued)

(*Continued*)

Action Two

Do you truly believe that your marketing strategy is consistent with and relevant to your target audience? Is it positioned well? Ask yourself: Does my customer really care?

Action Three

Does everyone on your team know what your marketing strategy is all about? And are they ready at the frontline to sell it to the customer?

Create Rhythm

CHAPTER

12

Routine = Rhythm = Revenue

"I figured if I had routine then I was in a position to put rhythm into the business. And this might just be our opportunity to stop walking in circles with one foot nailed to the floor and learn how to run!"

For nearly 20 years, my alarm went off at 5 A.M. each morning. Every day, I'd drag my sorry backside out of bed and try and get some exercise for a half hour. (Most days I would fail; some days I'd manage it only while on the phone to the other side of the world.) I'd grab a coffee and a quick bite to eat, jump in the car for the short ride to work—and then launch into the day.

I'd sort through messages, take calls, catch planes, speak, meet, greet, deal with staff, talk to customers, deal with lawyers, accountants, suppliers, and advisors. I was constantly running from place to place, meeting to meeting, call to call. Some 12 to 14 (and sometimes more) hours later, I would head home, eat dinner, and go looking for a glass of wine and a quiet spot to slump into a chair and stare at the TV.

Then I'd get up and do it all again the next day.

Monday would morph into Tuesday, which would then morph into Wednesday, then into next week, into next month, and next quarter—until all of a sudden I would find myself scrambling to get as much done as I could before the country shut down over the Christmas break. Come December 24, I could feel my whole body exhale as I knew I could enjoy a week of rest before we launched into the New Year and did it all again.

Christmas Eve would be a time to travel, and Christmas Day a time to spend with family. Even though I was exhausted from the year that had just ended, it signified another close to another business year. The days between December 25 and January 1 were a time to reflect on what had happened over the past year. Every year, I would sit on a beach somewhere for a week and ponder the blur that had been the last 12 months.

The process was always the same every year. Initially, I'd just be relieved to have a break. Then I would begin to reflect and become somewhat disappointed that the year wasn't as easy as I expected. Then I would just get frustrated with myself, and the same rush of thoughts would inevitably spill out. "I just wish I had more time, more money, more staff, more clients, more, I dunno ... something. We just never seem to get in front of it; we're always playing catch-up and we always seem to be spinning our wheels. It's just so frustrating. Why can't this get any easier? I'd just like one year when I didn't have to work so hard!"

Most years, I would find external reasons for why things did not seem to work out as planned. I blamed the government, the economy, our clients, the bank, our staff; there was always something or someone *else* messing things up.

At least, I thought there was—until

> I realized that it wasn't the circumstance or the situation
> that wasn't changing year in year out. It was *me* that wasn't
> changing.

I can remember the moment the blinding flash of the obvious hit me. I was sitting on the beach on the back tailgate of my Range Rover, dangling my toes in the sand and watching the waves. I had a cold beer in hand and a notebook sitting beside me. Only this time, instead of reflecting on the past 12 months, I decided to reflect on the previous three years. What did each of these years look like and what were the challenges we faced each year? What successes had we had and what failures had we weathered? And what led us to experience these things?

I did.

I was the business's leader, so I could be fairly certain that most of it was my doing. I was the one who kept leading us around in circles and diverting our focus toward new crusades for business or new positioning in the marketplace—always off on a quest for the next bright, shiny object.

The reason it never got any easier each year was because I never *made* it easier—for myself, or anyone else. I was spending every year busy, being busy, and I never took the time to determine how to make it easier. Sure, I would spend a week over Christmas reflecting. But then I'd simply launch myself—and the rest of the business—back into the same old grind. I was too focused on the business *day* ahead of me to take the time to think further into the future and the next business *decade*.

You see, if you can't make the time to develop a strategy to facilitate change in your businesses, then all you're doing is living the same day over and over again. If you put in the same effort with the same execution, you'll naturally get the same result. Why would you expect something would change if you are not doing anything to change it?

There are countless professionals who feel that there is simply not enough time. To overcome this obstacle, some of us have even attended weeklong seminars on time management. We've sat for hours on end to learn how to save time or make more time (something that has always appealed to my sense of humor. I sit for a week to work out how to save an hour ... ironic, isn't it?)

But it doesn't have to be that hard.

I realized on the beach that day that if my company was going to change, then *I* needed to change first. I had to get *me* focused and in mental shape before I could work on the business. And that meant that I had to develop some discipline in my daily schedule, find the time to make some modifications—because *my* actions define how everyone else in the business acts. If I am erratic and unfocused, then they will become erratic and unfocused. If I am busy being busy, then they will be the same. If I am darting from one focus to another, they will follow suit under the impression that this is simply lateral or creative thinking.

I figured that if I had a routine, then I was in a position to put *rhythm* into the business.

I needed to give the team a daily schedule of some sort to follow, so that they would come to work every day knowing what they were doing and what they needed to achieve, because it was written down and easy to follow. This way, maybe—just maybe—we'd stop running around like chooks without heads every day. And this might just be our opportunity to stop walking in circles with one foot nailed to the floor and finally learn how to run!

But it wasn't easy by any means. It took me a long time to get some personal rhythm going in my day before I could work on doing the same for the business, and then it took some years to get the right rhythm going in all of our companies. The following are some simple tactics I used to help create time and develop a better strategy to "give us our legs," so to speak.

The first and most important step was to ensure *I* had a daily rhythm. To this day, I set aside 30 minutes daily to clear my head and do my brain dump. I separate the things I can influence from the things I have influenced enough and the things I cannot influence in any way. I then answer the same three questions that I ask my team each morning: How did you do yesterday, what are you focused on today, and how are you going to do it better tomorrow? It just keeps me in check and ready to launch into the day with some rhythm and purpose. If you attach this basic daily activity to another daily habit or routine you have in your life, it's amazing how easy it becomes. I usually take these 30 minutes during my morning walk. I go through my mental checklist and then I try to focus on one topic or issue and hone in on some sort of desired outcome—no matter how small. I figure that if I can come up with one gem each day that facilitates change, then I have half a shot of the next day's not being Groundhog Day.

Some days I have a stroke of brilliance; others, I am as dumb as wood, and the best thought I can muster is how to rearrange my desk. And that's okay. As you go through this routine, don't feel like you have to change the world in a half hour; you just need to make a start at changing the world. You'll have days that you seem to be a modern-day genius, and others that you'll feel like you've been chugging vodka for breakfast.

Once you have *your* rhythm established, you can then work on the business. Once I felt I was in a groove we started to work on some simple rhythm in the business, and then as we got into a bit of a stride we added more "layers" that eventually became routine in our business day.

- **We introduced activity logs.** In other words, we disguised the concept of a time sheet with something we called an activity log. Be warned: Introducing this seemingly simple tool into your company will not be fun. If your employees are anything like mine, they will hate the idea and most likely want to stab you with a pen. But after about three months (and a bit of group therapy), they'll get over it. You'll certainly have to put up with screams along the way such as, "Why do I have to waste time doing activity logs?" or "This is crazy! I've got better things to do with my day!" But I actually went quite hard on this one; I was serious about getting us on track. I had everyone log their activity in 15-minute intervals on their computer calendar system. And then we shared calendars so I could see how everyone was going with their reporting and encourage them to keep on top of it. We also designated categories for the time each staff member spent and color-coded them with titles such as meetings, clients, travel, personal, administration, marketing, phone calls, and so on. While painful at first (especially for me), it became an invaluable tool that allowed us to see just how much time we were wasting as a business. It also gave us a great breakdown on individual efficiency.

The key to offsetting some of the staff moans and groans was for me to try the program before I introduced it to the team. And guess what? After three months of me personally giving the system a trial run first and then a further three months of staff trials, I found that yours truly was one of the worst offenders. I was wasting almost 30 percent of my time fluffing around in my office, shuffling papers, talking to mates on the phone, organizing Motorsport days at the track—generally not being very effective at all. I just didn't realize it until I wrote it down!

As a result of the findings from the logs in one of our companies, we even banned and blocked staff from instant messaging and social media sites, unless it was their core job focus in the business. Consider that for a moment; how much of a time suck do you think sites like those are on your business? I can tell you that it's pretty scary once you find out!

Another outcome of this exercise was that we were better able to understand what margin we were making on individual projects. Therefore, we could now allocate real hours to each project as opposed to guessing how long things took to execute. This, in turn, helped us immensely when calculating our real cost of seat for everyone.

The key to having everyone embrace the project was to be clear with them that its focus was not on working harder, just *smarter*. We also introduced our new and improved (and first successful) profit-sharing program for the staff to support the activity logs. That, coupled with the analysis of where and how we were spending our time, led them to a significant realization: Suddenly, time *was* money. *Their* money.

The overall result was that the staff became acutely aware of time and far more focused on how they spent their days. They aimed to maximize output, profit, and as a result, personal reward.

I still track my time and my efficiency on the days that I work, and it still allows me to get everything done in a much shorter period of time. I figure that if I save that 30 percent of my day that I used to waste and go a little harder on the days I *do* work, it means I can get my work done in three days a week, something that is a constant goal for me.

- **We began holding more meaningful meetings.** One of the other great outcomes from the activity logs was that they showed us just how unproductive our meetings were by highlighting their length and lack of output. We were also able to see just how many of those unproductive meetings we had each week or month.

So we adopted new meeting agendas that were shorter, sharper, and focused on specific outcomes. Each meeting had an elected chairperson whose role was not just to call and run the meeting but to ensure that we had a very clear agenda with specific items we were to cover—and that we all understood what we were to take away from the meeting. In some instances, we figured out that we didn't need a meeting at all by simply asking the chairperson what outcome he was seeking. The answer to that simple question helped us realize that we could solve the issue far more effectively with some one-on-one discussion.

This, in turn, offered us better time efficiency when we did meet. We even conducted some of our meetings standing so that people did not become complacent and comfortable. This kept the pace up nicely; everyone felt like they needed to keep moving or that they had somewhere else to go.

Pretty basic stuff really, but ask yourself: How many times do you accept a meeting invitation not really knowing why you are meeting in the first place? Or, how many times have you left a meeting only to have a discussion on the same topic at a meeting some weeks later, because there was no real outcome or plan of action that came from the last discussion?

- **We developed key team member daily updates.** One of the most significant outcomes from the meaningful meeting program was the inception of daily update meetings with key team members at 8:30 A.M. for about 5 to 10 minutes. If I was not in the office (and not speaking on a stage or on a plane), I would dial in for the meeting—no matter where I was in the world. The team would huddle around the speakerphone, and I would ask them three magic questions:

  1. How did you do yesterday?
  2. What are you focused on today?
  3. How are you going to do it better tomorrow?

These calls became legendary in the office. We nicknamed them our "Charlie Calls," because all the members of my key team at the time were female, and as I greeted them each morning on speakerphone they would answer in unison, "Morning, Charlie." Yeah, I know, quirky, but the *Charlie's Angels* connection made it a bit of fun!

The calls were helpful for me, as I typically did not need to call into the office again that day. They also forced everyone on my team to actually *think* about what they needed to deal with that day and to review their previous day to reflect upon whether they had achieved something of worth. It also guaranteed that we were moving forward each day and facilitating change in the business in some small way. It was a great mirror for all of us, and it quickly became apparent to me that this simple method—coupled with our company profit sharing program—allowed me to be out of the office for an average of 180-plus days a year without having to worry that things would go astray.

- **We developed recurring strategic planning time slots.** Now, this might sound simple at first; we all have strategic planning meetings, right? Well, while some businesspeople actually do hold the meetings, they don't always follow up on them. As a result, you end up conducting the same meeting in three months time (if, of course, you don't cancel it because you are all too busy). We identified this inefficiency from our activity logs, so we set about making our planning meetings more efficient, consistent, and productive.
- **We established monthly meetings that we called "administration strategy summits."** The agenda would last one to two hours, depending on what was happening in the business. We use this time to review matters like budgets, cash flow, debtors, and creditors with the entire team. Everyone in the group knows *all* the figures. I want them dialed into the business; after all, they are all on profit share.

From day one of implementation, these meetings would go ahead. Even if a client calls and requests to meet on that day at that appointed time, we say, "Sorry, we have a prior booking and can't make that time." Nobody ever minds. It's only when you disclose that the conflict is an internal meeting that clients will often request that you change it. This is why we prefer to tell them that it's a prior engagement—no details necessary. There is *nothing* more important to our team than planning. Without a strategic plan, there is no business; without business, there are clearly no clients. So strategic planning wins every time.

All team members are aware of what they need to bring to the meeting so we can assess the various metrics that need to be monitored. Each report is succinct and completed in a format with which they are all familiar so that we scan information quickly and efficiently.

- **We set out quarterly business planning strategy summits**. These meetings allow us to conduct what we call a "review/preview" session on our companies. How did we perform over the last three months of our businesses' development, and how are we going to perform in the next three months? The core focus is always on efficiency and business development. The sessions run for about three to four hours, and the outcome is an assessment of our key performance indicators (KPIs) for the next quarter.

On many occasions, I schedule these meetings to coincide with our advisory board meetings. This allows my team members to report some of their information to the board, and it allows the board to respond with suggestions on how my staff might handle future business issues.

To make sure that these sessions aren't all work and no play, I make room for some potential reward time. If we hit target for the quarter's KPIs, we take a few hours off and go and do something fun like spend the afternoon in a corporate box at the races or find a cool place for lunch somewhere.

- **We also introduced a twice-yearly two-day strategy retreat.** Our key team members travel to an off-site venue and spend two days locked in a room, planning the next six months—budgeting, marketing, administration, staffing, business development—we cover everything! All the information from these retreats goes straight into the business plan and gets entered live on-site to ensure that nothing is missed and that nothing we spoke about was strategic rhetoric. Usually, I'll book a penthouse on the beach someplace for us to have a place to work out of and a central recreation spot to kick back as well, so that these events have an element of fun that keeps us in a serious but relaxed environment.

We begin early each morning with a walk on the beach at dawn and a chat about anything that pops into our heads. When we get back to the apartment, I cook the team a big breakfast. It's coffee all round, and we get into it straightaway.

The day's agenda is split among the team members so that each has a topic and corresponding outcome to facilitate. This takes the load off me when preparing the retreat; they all have homework to do to prepare for the event, and they're all involved. This encourages them to buy into the process and own the results.

To keep us focused on the outcomes with purpose, we continue to ask ourselves these questions as the day goes on;

- Are we acting today to prepare for the better future?
- Will the action be profitable?
- Is the action in line with our company positioning, vision, and values?
- Are we keeping the next business cycle in mind to ensure we are following our *future-proofing* business philosophy?

We typically pound the agenda all morning, briefly pausing to make coffee or shove more confectionary or cookies into our faces. Then sometime around 2 P.M. we'll stop for a late lunch, and pull the cork out of a bottle of wine.

Actually, let me be honest and rephrase that; that's when *I* usually pull the cork out of a bottle of wine, because I have had enough for the day. At about this time, I often find myself staring out the window across the beach and into space like a bored puppy waiting for his master to get home with a new bone. My mind wanders from the agenda and onto thoughts of how I justify to myself the need for a new racecar or the new Porsche 911 GT3 that's just been released that week. As soon as another member of the team catches on to my lack of interest, he or she will, without prompting, head to the refrigerator to grab a bottle of my favorite white wine, exclaiming to the group that "Troy's gone!" and that it is clearly "wine o'clock."

The rest of the day is spent just hanging out as mates, learning more about each other, and discussing our vision and values in life. I occasionally give them a communication-starter question to answer designed to get them talking, something like, "Tell me about your favorite childhood memory." Anything that helps us learn more about each other.

In the evening, I cook dinner for them. It's kind of cool to have the boss cook for you and wait on you . . . my team seems to love it! We head back to our rooms and turn in fairly early each night and get up and do it all again the next day. We wrap up the retreat with a dinner out and the reward of a powerful two days of vision, focus, and *future-proofing*.

Key to all of these strategic planning activities is that we do not miss, nor delay, nor ignore a date we have set for the sessions. This guarantees that we spend time planning efficiently and effectively to make the strategy of the business more efficient and effective.

And all of a sudden, we have time.

Now, 10 years later, I average three days a week in the office, and spend the rest of my time writing, racing, resting, and retreating with my wife and my friends—all because our business is now more time-efficient than ever. It's the end result of a decade of time management and effective planning for a stronger future, and our total commitment to our business philosophy that everything we do today has a long-term effect on how well we *future-proof our business*.

But the reality is that it's not easy. And *you* have to make the first move to make it work.

Rhythm to Your Revenue!

Three things you need to do now to Future-Proof Your Business and to ensure you are more time-efficient.

Action One

Find your routine. The place to start is to find your 30 minutes for *you* each day. Your first habit is to make you more efficient and then put rhythm into the business. Remember: Your actions define how your staff will act. If you have no discipline with your time, then neither will they.

Action Two

Break the daily bad habits. Every time you feel like you are shuffling papers, being ineffective, wasting time, being indecisive or just messing around, stand up. Just stand up at your desk until you clear your head, regroup, and go back to work. Take notice of how often that happens in your day. If you can keep track of the time you spend on your feet, it will tell you how much time you waste in a day, even without looking at your calendar.

Action Three

Now translate that time into *real* time. Consider what you could achieve if you used the time you were wasting by productively developing strategy so you had clarity and vision for the future. Think about it.

Lead the Revolution

Change or Die!

"No matter what you have read in the previous pages, the one thing that will stop you from facilitating change in your life and your business is your fear of change itself."

My wife and I are sitting on a flight from Florida to California. It's the first leg of one of our regular journeys across the country before we head across the Pacific to Australia.

This trip is a longer than usual commute across the United States to our Australian home Down Under, but it's not nearly as tough as it used to be when I first started in business. We sit and chat and have our usual "board meeting" on the plane, as we enjoy the time without phones or the Internet. We hit the first class lounge at LAX and spend the 6 hours in transit preparing for the last 14-hour leg. A shower and a meal later, we enjoy a few glasses of champagne as we watch the passing tourists and business travelers come and go. We chat about everything from the next marketing campaign to our potential future children's names.

My wife and I love this time. It's an opportunity for us to jump out of the tornado that our lives become from time to time and look from the outside in. It gives us a chance to reflect on our purpose and to realign our personal visions and plans in preparation for the next chapter of life. It's when we look back on our achievements over recent months and make plans for the future.

I've spent some time reading over this manuscript on this particular trip. I've been talking to my wife about what stories I may have forgotten to put in along the way, as I pondered the last 20 years of my life.

It's funny; some days I feel like it's just been one big blur, while on others, I can vividly recall the details and blow by blow, year by year experiences. Today, after such an amazing year of change, one moment in time that comes to mind is a conversation I had in Tokyo over a decade ago.

After my first EO board meeting in Tokyo, I had collared a fellow member with whom I seemed to connect. He was clearly a focused and talented businessperson, who had done very well in a technology business he owned. After our formal board dinner had finished, I approached him and asked if he'd like to head downstairs for a beer. My intent, of course, was to pick his brain on how he had done so well in such a short period of time in his entrepreneurial career.

So we hit the bar, and after hearing his life story over about 400 beers and 3,000 sakes, along the way scribbling countless notes on napkins, the night was finally drawing to a close. I could tell that we should be winding down, because our speech was beginning to sound more and more like *we were* Japanese.

My last brain suck finally arrived at about 2 A.M., when I realized that I had to find a way to sum up all of my newfound knowledge, and I posed my last question. "So, if you had a single gem to give me, what would it be? What's the one thing that you could pinpoint in your business career that has helped you become so successful to date?" My new friend slowly turned to me as he pulled a napkin from the other side of the bar, and said, "I run my life and my business on three words: Change or die."

I paused, looked at the words he'd written on the napkin, and looked up at him. I simply said, "Wow mate, that's a bit harsh . . . okay, so, I got that . . . what else?"

He drank the last of his beer, put his empty bottle on the bar, turned to me, and with a little more conviction this time, said, "You don't get it. You asked me for one gem; I've given it to you. That's the gem; that's all you need to know. I'm done. I'm off to bed." And on that note, he left me standing at the bar.

I paid the tab, and once again I retreated to my room and stood in the dark staring over the lights of Tokyo for what seemed like hours. I kept repeating the words in my head, "I change, I'm sure I change, yeah I change, I'm almost certain I change." And then, in a moment of truth and reality, the words slowly came out of my mouth into the cool Japanese night: "No . . . I don't."

On the way home in the plane the next day, I made one promise to myself: to go home and change one thing and one thing only. And as you've already read, that was a *good* thing—considering I stepped off the plane and walked straight onto a life-turned-movie set that was a mix of *Armageddon* and *Independence Day*.

I solidified my commitment to change by coining this phrase in our company's strategic plan:
Change is not an action; it's a consciousness.

They were easy words to say, but oh so *very* hard to actually execute. In fact, it took me a long time to get the rhythm of change into the business. It was on *my* mind on a daily basis; the hard part was to put it into everyone else's consciousness.

In the years that followed, I found that I was continually checking myself to ensure I was facilitating change in the business every day, even if in a very small way.

As I sit in the airport lounge on my way home on this trip, my brain fast-forwards a handful of years to a conversation I had in North Queensland with my father and his wife Elizabeth. I was having one of those "thank God for a few days off" moments, sitting at the bar in their house on a warm summer evening with a glass of my favorite New Zealand Sauvignon Blanc and reflecting on the past few years. Despite the incredible support I had received from my family and close friends, the many twists and turns I'd experienced in that time were prompting me to question aloud why I'd faced so many challenges.

After a pause, Elizabeth said quietly, "You needed to do all of those things in order to get you where you are today, to bring you to this point in life. This is what you were *meant* to do." I must have looked at her with an inquisitive expression, because she continued. "Had you not been a radio announcer, you might not have had the skills to be a public speaker. Had you not had so many business interests and experiences, you might not have had a story to tell on stage; and had you not faced the diversity and adversity you have, well, then you might not have had the wisdom to share. This is what you were meant to do—to share your story with others."

I left North Queensland and pondered that conversation the whole way home. I'm sure that many others had said something similar to me over the years, and I'm sure that this was not the first time I had thought about it, but this was for sure the first time I took notice, probably because now I was ready to take notice. I had a bit of a chuckle to myself. Yup, things in life happen for a reason.

I knew in my heart that I truly loved being on stage sharing stories with an audience, and I enjoyed writing about my business and life experiences. The simple fact that the stories

resonated with others gave me a sense of purpose. It struck me
that if I was to get serious about making this a life-changing
experience, and to follow that purpose, then I needed to once
again change my life. And while it took me some time to make
the changes in my business life so I might focus on spending
more time speaking and writing, it was a change that I am so
glad I made.

So here I am today, sitting with my wife, pondering what
the next significant transformation in our life is going to be.
This time, we decide it's our commitment to stay longer in the
United States and continue our adventure.

For me, it's a fairly big deal to make a personal commitment
to do my best to inform and inspire others to be the best they
can be by sharing some of my stories as openly as I can to help
them on their way, but I am inspired by the many people that
did the same for me so many years ago. And that leads me to the
last of the things I can share with you to help you *future-proof
your business*.

1. **Be aware**—and truly understand *you*. Know your true values, your vision, your personal desires in life, and have
   clarity of a plan to achieve all of those things to offer you a
   sense of purpose and personal satisfaction.

2. **Understand**—how you want your business to fit into the
   life you want to lead. You run your business, it does not run
   you. Remember, business runs in cycles. The key to making
   your business a more efficient tool to create wealth that will
   fund your personal plan is to understand those cycles and
   to *truly* understand how to create a more resilient business
   around them.

3. **Learn**—Listen to the stories and lessons of others. It does
   not matter if the lesson is good or bad; all are opportunities for you learn how to become a better person. People
   come into your life for a reason, a season, or a lifetime.

Understand their message in your life and be aware of their presence, and you will gather so much more information to help you in your journey to create a better future.

Always check yourself and make sure that you are truly and consistently being honest with yourself, and that you are following your personal plan, your values, your vision, and your purpose. And if you find that you're not, change accordingly so that you can return to the true path you wish to set yourself for the future and live each day with purpose. Business became so much easier for me once I really understood *me*, and what I wanted business to mean to me.

Future-proofing is not about being a leading global economic forecaster, Nobel-prize–winning visionary, noted prophet, or world-class psychic. It's not about predicting the future, it's about having a better understanding and awareness of how everything you do *today* changes your future.

Future-proofing is not about changing who you are, it is about understanding who you are, to be the real and true you and in turn create a real and true business.

Future-proofing is not about making a dramatic change in your life, it's about changing the way you approach everything that influences you in life.

I believe *future-proofing* is as easy as understating how to apply a handful of easy personal disciplines to know you are embracing the opportunity for change in life such that change becomes a consciousness, not just an action.

Remember in order to *future-proof* your business you must first *future-proof* yourself.

And my last tip before I leave you. No matter what you have read in the previous pages, the one thing that will stop you from facilitating any change in your life and your business is your fear of change itself.

Good luck in the future!

The Revolution of Change!

Three things you need to do now to Future-Proof Your Business and make sure you are really getting real and getting down to business!

Action One

Are you constantly looking at what change you can facilitate *today* to ensure a better future for your *tomorrow*?

Action Two

What do you do each day to ensure you are really, truly aware of your surroundings and the impact of that on your life and your business?

Action Three

What habits have you incorporated into your life and your business to keep you in check with your personal plan, vision, values, and your purpose?

YOUR PERSONAL WORKBOOK

Real-Life Strategies to Prepare Your Business
for Tomorrow, Today

Now It's Time for You

To get real, and get down to business.

Chapter 1 The Lesson of Learning

Reflect on the four core bad business beliefs that will stop you from future-proofing your business. How are you going to eliminate them from your life?

1. You *can* make **time**:

_____

_____

_____

_____

2. It's *not* **different** for you:

_____

_____

_____

_____

3. It's okay to **ask**; have no fear:

_____

_____

_____

_____

4. Seek **vision**, and purpose will come:

_____

_____

_____

_____

Chapter 2 Truth and Reality versus Fear and Greed

The Truth Test

Is it perception or reality? Are you dealing with the real issue at hand or just the perceived issue on the surface? Dig a little deeper; you might find that there's more to it and that the *real* issue can be traced back to your own actions.

Ask yourself—What's the real issue I'm facing?

_____

_____

_____

_____

Claim not blame. Claim responsibility for *everything*. It's *your* business, and you are responsible for its success or failure. So take control. And if (or rather, when) you *do* make a mistake, put your hand on your heart and say, "Yup, I screwed up—and here's how I'm going to fix it." Confident leaders admit mistakes in truth and have confidence that they can fix them.

Ask yourself—What mistakes have I made recently that it is my job to correct?

_____

_____

_____

_____

Share the issues with staff; if they can see it, they can help solve it. Let your staff know about the problems you're dealing with, and the reality of the situations at hand. They can only help you solve them if they know the issues exist.

Ask Yourself—What current issues can you share with your staff?

_____

_____

_____

_____

Listen to yourself first, then listen to others. It's easy to find experts around you; they'll be the ones who are first to tell you they know better. You know the ones—they start their sentences with phrases like, "You should . . .," "Why don't you . . .," or "How come you haven't . . . ?" You know when you are not in touch with your truth. Stop and listen to your intuition talking to you first.

What is your intuition telling you that you may have been ignoring?

_____

_____

_____

_____

Truth or fear. Before you make that key decision or action, ask yourself this simple question: Are you making the decision in truth or fear?

Chapter 3 Make Time to Make It Easier

Your Brain Dump Journal

Brain Dump (include the date)

Things I can influence today:

Things I have influenced enough and need to set aside:

Things I can no longer influence nor will allow to take up space in my mind:

_____

_____

_____

_____

Chapter 4 The Value of Vision

Part 1 of the Vision: My Personal Plan

- What do I want to be when I grow up?
- What do I want to represent?
- What is my real purpose?
- How do I propose to fulfill these things in my life?

_____

_____

_____

_____

Part 2 of the Vision: My Life Plan

- What will my legacy be?
- How does this legacy apply to my family?
- How does it interact with my personal purpose?
- What can I do to help those close to me in their journey to fulfill their purpose?

_____

_____

_____

_____

Part 3 of the Vision: My Business Plan

- I believe that my business is my own personal economic driver. It helps me achieve my life vision, and it provides for me and those who count on me.
- I must build my business on truth and reality to succeed.

- I run my business; it does not run me.

_____

_____

_____

_____

Part 4 of the Vision: My People Plan

- There is no such thing as a self-made millionaire. Businesses, wealth, and good fortune are built with the help of good people.
- If I am to engage others for help, I need to understand them first.
- How can my business help others achieve their visions?
- What milestones will keep my business vision and beliefs in check?

_____

_____

_____

_____

Chapter 5 The Need to Lead

Some questions to keep yourself in check as a leader:
- Are you a confident or arrogant leader; in other words, do you lead based on ability or ego?
- Do you lead in truth and reality or fear and greed?
- Do you show your vulnerability and display your needs to those you lead? Are you open with others?
- Are you learning while you teach?

- Do you offer experiences or advice and opinions?
- Do you make rules in your business and then not follow them, yet expect others to?
- Do you ask others to observe a routine or process, yet don't follow one yourself?
- Do you manage by example (truth and reality) or instruction (ego and fear)?
- Do you show interest in those you lead so that they may show interest in you?
- Are you aware of your evolution as a leader?

_____

_____

_____

_____

Chapter 6 I'm Done!

Develop your own exit formula.

- What is the life cycle of this business category? Where is my company currently positioned in that cycle?

_____

_____

_____

_____

- What are the triggers for the "fun factor" in the business?

_____

_____

_____

_____

202 Future-Proofing Your Business

• How quickly can I add value to the business?

_____

_____

_____

_____

• How much is enough?

_____

_____

_____

_____

Chapter 7 The Information Age

Information comes at us in so many ways—so how are you going to collect it?

The price I am prepared to pay for information:
• What information do I need?
• Where am I going to get it?
• What will my budget be to gather this information?
• How will I keep the gathering of information a discipline in the business?
• When am I going to start ?

_____

_____

_____

_____

Networks to join:
- Where do I find them?
- What value will they be to me and my business?
- Who can introduce me to that network?
- What does my elevator pitch sound like?

_____

_____

_____

_____

Groups or organizations to join:
- Where do I find them?
- What value will they be for me and my business?
- Who can introduce me to that group or organization?
- How can I really get involved in the group or organization?

_____

_____

_____

_____

Learning events to attend:
- What do I want to learn this year?
- What value will that provide for me personally? What value will it provide for the company?

_____

_____

_____

_____

Courses to take:

- What will be complementary to the other information I am gathering?
- When am I going to take these courses? What will I do to make the time to take them?
- What will these courses cost?

_____

_____

_____

_____

Information to write down:

- How am I going to capture the information I've learned?
- What am I going to do with it once I have captured it?
- How can I pass this information on to my team?

_____

_____

_____

_____

Chapter 8 Strategy that Sticks

Give yourself a moment to scratch down some notes on what you would put into your strategic planning document (see Figure WB.1). Some key things you should consider are:

- Executive overview
- Business strategy
- Operations strategy

Issue	Focus	Objective	Action	Outcome	Who	When
We number issues for reference, because there may be a few action items for the same issue.	What is the core thing we're addressing with this part of the strategy? (Give it a title as a reference.)	What are we trying to achieve by addressing this particular issue?	What is the core thing we are going to do to make a change and tackle this issue?	What desired outcomes are we seeking by addressing this issue?	Who is going to be responsible for handling this change in the business?	When are we going to have this complete? (This may include creating progress milestones along the way.)

Figure WB.1   Your Strategic Plan Action Grid

- Human relations/people strategy
- Marketing strategy
- Financial strategy

Chapter 9 The Rewards of Rewards

Step 1

In order for you to develop a structured reward scheme for your business, you need to understand those who you are rewarding first.

- What are their hot buttons—or the things driving them to do their best? Is it money, personal gratification, time off, gifts, or a clear path to leadership in the business? What is important to *them*?

- How often do you feel you need to reward your employees to keep them focused in the workplace—weekly, monthly, quarterly, annually?
- Do you reward them as individuals, as a group, or both?

_____

_____

_____

_____

Step 2

What are the metrics of your reward scheme? How are you going to structure it so that it is easy to understand without interpretation or potential interference?

- How can you handcuff your team together in the workplace?
- What can you do to truly integrate your teams so they have appreciation for each other?
- How are you going to then integrate your reward scheme into your daily operations in the business? Does something need to change to accommodate this integration?
- What are *you* going to do to show discipline in the workplace?

_____

_____

_____

_____

Step 3

How much are you prepared to share with your team? The more you can show your team how they are going to reach their reward targets, the easier it is for them to feel like they are going to achieve this.

Consider adopting the following parameters:

- Open-book management, including your salary package.
- Regular disclosure of general profit and loss to show business profitability, or potential cash flow challenges.
- Create a collaborative approach to the development of sales budgets for the business.

_____

_____

_____

_____

Chapter 10 Show Me the Money

A bigger business costs bigger bucks, so ask yourself these questions:

- How can you alter your supply chain to shorten debtor days from clients and to speed up supply from your vendors?
- Are your growth plans realistic? Have you forecast using an aggressively optimistic model based on *ego*? Or did you use a conservatively honest and sensible model based on *ability*?
- What planning time have you set aside for understanding your financial position?

- Are you showing discipline by sticking to that plan, or are you cutting corners on the time you spend planning for finances?
- What metrics are you using to assess and manage your company's monetary issues?
- Are you focused on sales or profit?
- Are you taking personal responsibility for your financial position in the business?
- Are you thinking about what money you need in the business *first* and then considering *how* you are going to make that money—and planning accordingly?

_____

_____

_____

_____

Chapter 11 Meaningful Marketing

What does your current business positioning look like in the eyes of your customers?

_____

_____

_____

_____

What is your desired business positioning?

_____

_____

_____

_____

Keeping this information in mind, are you clear you are hitting your customers' hot buttons?

_____

_____

_____

_____

What do you need to change to create your desired business positioning?

_____

_____

_____

_____

What are the key elements to your marketing strategy?

Brand

_____

_____

_____

_____

Area

_____

_____

_____

_____

Relationship

_____

_____

_____

_____

Local

_____

_____

_____

_____

Information Technology

_____

_____

_____

_____

Training

_____

_____

_____

_____

Chapter 12 Routine = Rhythm = Revenue

What can you do to create rhythm and become more efficient and effective in your business?

Daily

_____

_____

_____

_____

Weekly

_____

_____

_____

_____

Monthly

_____

_____

_____

_____

Quarterly

_____

_____

_____

_____

Biannually

_____

_____

_____

_____

Annually

_____

_____

_____

_____

Chapter 13 Change or Die!

Your commitment for change:
- To be aware
- To understand
- To learn

_____

_____

_____

_____

Your strategy for change:
- To be aware
- To understand
- To learn

_____

_____

_____

_____

Your daily routine for change:
- To be aware
- To understand

- To learn

_____

_____

_____

_____

ABOUT THE AUTHOR

There are theory specialists and then there are those who have been there. Troy Hazard, business expert with over 20 years' experience, has survived moments of both success and sheer desperation in business. Drawing from a lifetime of innovative, real-life business and leadership experience, he now shares these stories around the world.

There are few situations in the business world that Troy has not experienced and survived—from massive financial loss to stunning success. The serial entrepreneur, who has founded and nurtured 10 businesses over two decades, Troy has been a few days from bankruptcy, has turned around businesses that were suffering enormous losses, and has consulted to countless successful companies across the planet.

These talents have earned him international respect, so much so that he was elected by the world's foremost business leaders for the role of 2006–2007 global president of the elite Entrepreneurs' Organization, a role he says was one of his greatest challenges.

He is a Certified Speaking Professional, has cohosted two national network business television shows, and is a regular business commentator in the press and on network radio and television across the United States.

His simple philosophy on how to *future-proof your business*:
"*Business happens in cycles. Your ability to manage these cycles successfully lies in how you interpret information from the past and deal with it in the present, to be more resilient through cycles of the future.*"